OF CRAB, CUCUM

E. SALAD OF KING

POTATOES, GREEN BEA

D TRUFFLE. ROASTED Y

ND CONFIT. TOMATO SA

E OF ATLANTIC SALMO

ATOES WITH CRAYFISH

D SILVER PERCH, OSIE

ND CRISPY CELERY, CL

SE OF ROCK FISH, CROC

D SAFFRON TORTELLIN

ES AND CHAMPAGNE C

OES ASPARAGUS, AND

F OF RABBIT CONFITS

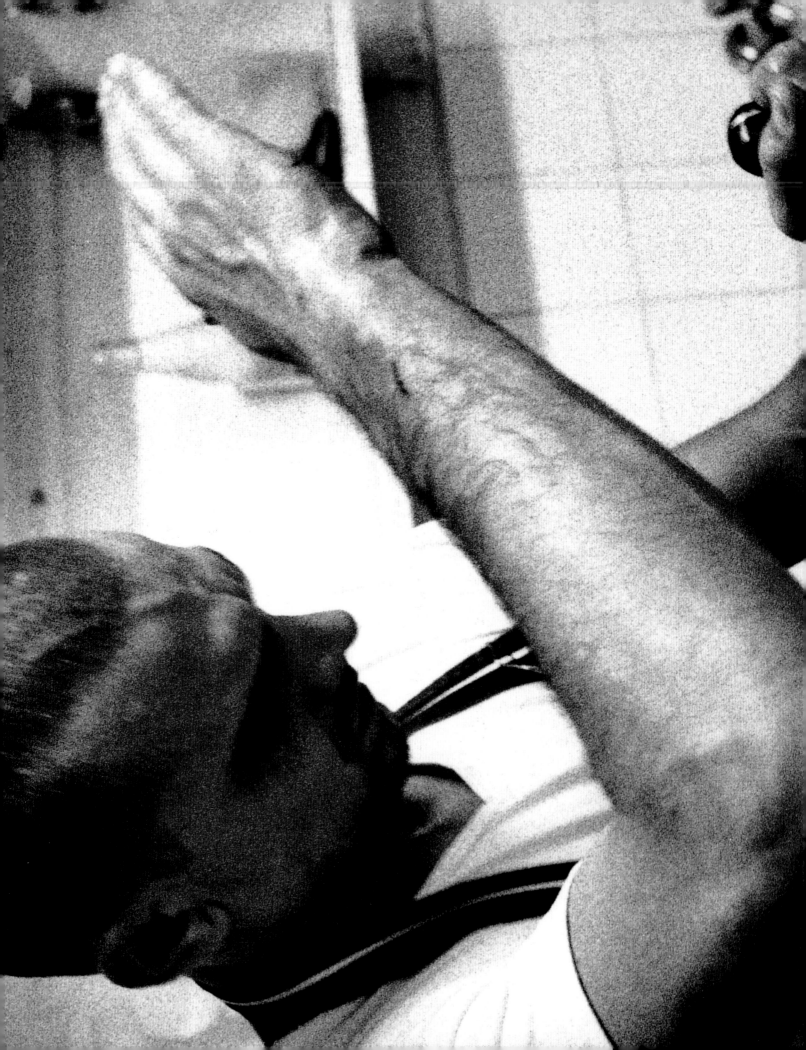

ESTESTESTEST COOKBOOK

MARRIAGES

PHOTOGR

DONOVAN COOKE & PHILIPPA SIBLEY-COOKE

APHY SIMON GRIFFITHS

DESIGN VISNJA BRDAR

NH
NEW HOLLAND

EST EST EST COOKBOOK MARRIAGES

For our parents
Bet and Sib, Val and Donovan

There are so many aspects to *Marriages*.

It's a love story, the history of a restaurant, a recipe book and a diner's guide to what goes on behind the scenes. A before and after glimpse of the food that is on the table. It is also about a unique mix of talent and passion: the cooking abilities of Donovan Cooke and Philippa Sibley-Cooke, and Frank Heaney's passion for wine and restaurants. When you talk to them about how and why they started in the hospitality business and how hard they worked over the years, the amazing successes that are est est est and Luxe seem natural. But the question to ask is why there aren't more businesses like theirs. And that is the key to the book. What makes for successful marriages and restaurants is the ability to 'marry'…to be able to work together, to combine talents, to respect each other's integrity. Then the taste and judgement to be able to make the mix transcend each of its fundamental elements, that is, to make the sum greater than the parts. It's also what great cooking is about. Getting the basic ingredients right, knowing how to combine them, having the patience and technique to work them perfectly and then being able to taste and judge the result. These qualities are the stuff of greatness. They are rare. The late, great chef Alain Chapel wrote a book called *La cuisine, c'est beaucoup plus que des recettes* (Cooking is much more than recipes). *Marriages* is about just that.

Mietta O'Donnell

The year we got married Donovan and I were living and working in a small village called Joigny in France. It was a difficult year, but a significant one for us: Donovan rediscovered what was important to him as a chef and I gained real confidence in my professional abilities. We also found out just how well we worked as a team. More significantly, that was where est est est was conceived.

'We lived in a tiny attic flat' sounds romantic, but it wasn't. Our place in Joigny was uncomfortable and underfurnished. We worked long hours and even though we were in a Michelin-starred restaurant we were broke because I didn't have a work visa and wasn't getting paid. There wasn't much to do between shifts so we would sit at our dining-table, our only real piece of furniture, drink wine and talk.

And we used to plan. We'd dream up menus and make up dishes and we'd talk about the kind of restaurant we wanted to run. We knew we couldn't afford to have our own place back in London – not of the calibre of the places we'd been working at – and we didn't want to go back to working for someone else there. That would not only have meant a lack of freedom to implement our dreams but also a resumption of our previous lives spent like miners in hell. Kitchens in London are mostly underground so there are no windows. The enormous stoves are faintingly hot; and you started cooking for lunch and dinner at 8 a.m. and worked until 1 a.m. The work space was extremely limited, and within it were crammed teams of overworked, overtired and obsessive people who do not remember the light of day, working in close proximity, six days a week. With only one day off a week, most of us gave in to the insane inclination to make the most of it and partied hard. When we left London for France we looked like the grass that grows under a bucket that's been left on the lawn for too long – pale, unnatural-looking and near death.

After our twelve months in France I really wanted to go home to Australia. Donovan wasn't convinced but for my sake he agreed to 'have a look'. The first six months in Melbourne were horrendous: we were knocking on doors thinking that we'd get work without a problem because of our experience, but instead were told that people didn't want our style of food. The search for an establishment that was more concerned with offering quality food than conforming to gastronomic fashion eventually led us to Mietta's restaurant. To our relief Mietta provided Donovan with an excellent introduction to Melbourne; not only was she incredibly supportive but working there allowed us the freedom to begin developing the sort of dishes and menus we'd talked about in Joigny. Working in Melbourne's finest dining room certainly speeded up the process of making it onto the culinary map too; Mietta's gave us the profile we needed to succeed on our own.

est est est opened its doors about eighteen months after Frank Heaney, our partner who oversees the dining room, called Donovan out of the blue one really busy night at Mietta's. He wanted to know if we were interested in opening a restaurant with him. Donovan said 'we're busy' and hung up on him. Months later, when Mietta decided to close her restaurant, Frank rang again. This time we were ready to consider his proposal seriously. After a year of hunting and negotiating for the right place, est est est was finally launched. Two years later Donovan and I opened our second place, Luxe.

Having our own places has given us the freedom to do things the way we want to, completely. We know that a good dining experience in a restaurant is about much more than just the food, but for us, the food is the focus. When we come up with dishes, testing and perfecting them, our primary concern is about capturing the essence of the primary ingredients, using combinations that enhance and highlight rather than those that obscure. This simple philosophy is carried through to the dining room: we do not have a lot of decoration, the service is prompt but never intrusive, we serve our food on plain white plates and our wine in the best glasses. It is the food that we want people who dine at est est est to remember.

Philippa Sibley-Cooke

A DAY AT EST EST EST

Stripped bare, the kitchen at est est est would look poky. This is not a kitchen like those you see in the pages of a magazine or cookbook. It is furnished with the necessary equipment to do eighty-odd covers a night and supply Luxe, Philippa and Donovan's other restaurant, and there is nothing delicate or pretty about the equipment — it is battered, and everything is made from plastic or metal. (There's a reason for that — glass breaks when thrown.) That the eight people who work here can fit into the space, let alone function effectively, is quite a stretch. In the centre is the main work bench and beside that is the stainless steel table used for plating up the food. Behind the bench, along the wall, is the stove. This has two sets of four open-flame burners. Joshua and Ben work on either side of Donovan in the space between the central work bench and the stove. In this space that is just wide enough to allow the oven doors to be opened, the three pivot between the two work surfaces to turn out most of the entrées and all of the main dishes: Donovan and Joshua are on the meat and seafood and Ben is on the vegetables and garnishes. All the food necessary for service is stored in a fridge as it is freshly prepared each day — the meat and seafood all trimmed and portioned; the sauces finished; the pasta, pastries and extra vegetables and garnishes all ready to go. Everything is carefully arranged so that it is clearly visible and readily accessible for fast and easy extraction. Through a door between the stove and the main sink area is the cold larder where Karen helps Philippa to produce all of the pastry and desserts for est est est and some for Luxe. This room contains an oven, another fridge, two work benches and a cooling rack. During service the apprentice, Joseph — or Jethro, as he's known — works where he's needed; he may be at the plating-up table, in the cold larder constructing entrées, serving up the appetisers or preparing more herbs or vegetable garnishes if they run out. There is no room in this kitchen for anything superfluous other than to produce food.

8.00 a.m. Joseph arrives and checks the veal stock, which is always the last thing put on to gently cook overnight. He has come in a little earlier to let in the man who'll fix the vacuum-pack machine, which broke down last night while Donovan was doing the pigeons. It's needed today to package portions of lamb navarin for Luxe. The kitchen there does lunch and dinner, so there's no time or room for the long slow cooking required for this dish. **9.30 a.m.** Donovan and Philippa arrive. Donovan looks tired – the World Cup is on, and being screened in the early hours of the morning. The radio is turned on and they change into their work clothes: pants, some once-white T-shirts and blue-and-white striped aprons. Everyone in the kitchen wears the same gear. **10.00 a.m.** All of the kitchen staff are now here and are starting to go about the business of preparing for the night's service. Donovan inspects the fish delivery which has just arrived. All seems to be OK. **10.30 a.m.** The meat arrives. As usual Donovan looks through the delivery. Something's up: 'F***in'…this lamb's wrong.' He's on the phone to the butcher. Not very many words are spoken, then 'Right then,' before he hangs up. 'He's on his way over.' Donovan goes back to filleting fish. His pace is fast and steady, but he's clearly not happy. Everyone else is working at the same pace. The little chitchat that was taking place before has come to a complete stop. **11.00 a.m.** The butcher bustles through the back door wearing his suit (it's his day off), has a few apologetic words for Donovan and, still in his suit, proceeds to saw up the lamb forequarters he's brought to replace the lot that was delivered earlier. Donovan had visited them yesterday to explain how he wanted the meat portioned, but some misunderstanding had occurred with a temporary staff member, which meant the lamb was cut too small for the navarin. Before too long the problem is fixed. **1.00 p.m.** It's heads down all round. Things are running behind schedule today. The fish stock which normally goes on at midday for 20 minutes has only just hit the stovetop. Donovan is not pleased, 'So far everything I've done today has been for Luxe…I've picked a fine stage in my career to give up drinking.' **1.30 p.m.** Ben is deglazing the pans in which the ingredients for the veal stock have been roasting. Everyone in the kitchen must learn to make perfect stocks and they're Ben's responsibility at the moment. Donovan explains: 'The most important thing they have to learn here is stocks – it's what gets chefs bollocked the most, because if a stock is shit then the sauce is shit and if the sauce is shit, then I'm shit.' **2.00 p.m.** Lunchtime. Every day, without fail, the staff sit down to lunch together. Not only is it important that they eat a proper meal to get them through the rigours of service, it provides training. Today Jethro has made gnocchi and veal shanks and Joshua has done the sauce. **3.00 p.m.** Josh rolls out long sheets of pasta for the ravioli and tortellini. He takes a little mousse from the fridge and poaches some to test it. He tastes, offers it to Donovan and then to Philippa. Donovan says, 'More salt.' Philippa nods. Josh adjusts the mousse, poaches some more and they all taste again. Perfect. He then sets about making ninety perfectly plump tortellini. **3.20 p.m.** Ben is straining the fish stock, Josh is lining a terrine mould with bacon and Joseph is chopping a huge pile of shallots. In the cold larder Karen takes a lemon tart from the oven and Philippa is assembling pithiviers. Everyone, including Donovan, is doing his or her own dishes. The kitchen hands don't start until 4.00. **4.00 p.m.** A change in the atmosphere comes with the first sign of the countdown to service. The sauces are brought out. Donovan warms some of each to test them and gets Josh to as well (for training rather than confirmation). He makes some minor adjustments to one or two. These are all clearly labelled and lined up: he tells the story of a night when the sauce for the lamb went on a fish dish. An error such as this may seem like a mere irritation, but the implications were wide-ranging – all of the dishes for that table had to be held back (how to keep them warm without spoiling them?) while the fish was re-cooked. All of the other orders down the line were delayed by vital minutes. Joseph picks and chops the herbs. These are never done earlier so that they're perfectly fresh and fragrant. **4.25 p.m.** Ben continues to prepare the garnishes, using his asbestos fingers to stir the shallots and garlic he's sweating off in a pan for the pomme boulangère. He slices the potatoes on the mandolin and sets about making sixteen perfect potato mandalas. **5.30 p.m.** Donovan seals the bags of navarin for Luxe, each with one serve of meat and some sauce. Once sealed, it's ready to go: 'It's perfect because it's easy to store. Then you just heat in water and serve, and it comes out exactly as it is now; it doesn't dry out.' **5.45 p.m.** Frank pins the list of bookings to the wall. The first booking is for 6.30, the last is at 9.30. Eighty-four people all up, twenty-four tables. These are purposely staggered so that diners receive their food in good time and the kitchen is not so over-stressed that standards start to fall, or waiting times increase. However, between 8.00 and 8.30 is when the most people are due. Frank briefs Philippa and Donovan on which regulars are in and which politicians or celebrities. Philippa explains who's who when necessary. Josh stocks the kitchen fridge. Meats have been trimmed and portioned. He measures out individual serves of mussels and deep-sea clams, complete with a little juice for the roasted hapuka: 'We're far too busy to do this later on.' **6.15 p.m.** The music is turned off. On Donovan's bench is a slab of the finest quality French butter which he uses for finishing sauces to order. Donovan briefs Josephine, Philippa's sister, who does the pass on most evenings. He tells her which dishes the staff should be promoting, and to encourage people to be adventurous in their choices so that he can continue to serve interesting dishes. This way, he can make sure that the things he never keeps overnight like the stuffed pastas and fish are all sold and not wasted. The person who does the pass is the single point of communication between the front of house and the kitchen: it's her job to post the orders taken by the waiters, keep track of what each table is up to, and to let Donovan know when the diners are ready for the next stage of their meal. Throughout the evening they relay messages to staff about the availability of limited dishes and call for service the instant before a table's food is ready to go out. **6.10 p.m.** After the steady industry of the day, the kitchen seems unnaturally quiet. The benches are being cleaned and everything is put away or laid out in readiness for the next few hours. Truffle oil, chive tips, Celtic salt, fines herbs and chervil sprigs go on the plating-up table. For the first time the whir of the fans is noticeable. **6.20 p.m.** Everyone flicks a pointless look at the speaker on the wall as it beeps to announce the arrival of the first customers. Donovan says, 'That's the sound of Armageddon.' Then, 'Soups ready, Jethro'. He swings his arms around and jumps up and down like a boxer before a fight. The atmosphere is tense, fingers that haven't stopped all day are now drumming the benches. More waiters start arriving and squeeze through to the change area. Apart from their quiet enquiries, nobody is talking. **6.30 p.m.** There's a palpable easing of tension as the first order comes in. Donovan pins it to the tacked-together board above his bench. 'Ça marche! Tortellini, mushroom, trout, veal, hare, hapuka…rock, rock, rock.' Joseph does the appetiser, Jerusalem artichoke soup served in coffee cups. Joshua takes the pasta, meat and fish from the fridge and lays them down in order. The kitchen is busy again but the nature of the action has changed – this is fast and furious. The appetisers are carried out to the dining room. **6.45 p.m.** In the cold larder Philippa dots vinaigrette around a precarious little tower of trout, avocado and Kipfler potatoes. Donovan brushes a pithivier with truffle oil as Joseph dresses a plate in readiness for this and another for the tortellini. Josh passes the pasta and bugs to Ben who arranges them on the plate; sauce is frothed and spooned around. Philippa gives the lot a once over, making minor adjustments as Josephine calls for service. **6.50 p.m.** Donovan is sealing veal in a pan on top of the stove. It will go into the oven to finish cooking and rest just long enough so that it's perfect when it leaves the kitchen. The door buzzer goes. Activity dies down again as all wait for the next order to come through and for the first table to be ready for their mains. **7.00 p.m.** Next order. A flurry of activity follows 'Trout, ravioli, Dory, pigeon, hare'. Beeps from the door. **7.10 p.m.** No break in the action: 'Ravioli, trout, tortellini, two dory, hapuka, pigeon.' The next order follows hot on the heels of the last one. **7.15 p.m.** A man who didn't order an entrée changes his mind once he sees his companion's tortellini. This is fast-tracked. Philippa queries why one table's mains are going out so soon after their entrées have been cleared. Josephine: 'They have to be out by 9 o'clock.' Another waiter arrives and calls out the soccer results in response to Donovan's query. **7.30 p.m.** Only half of the booking for fifteen people at 7.15 has arrived. The pressure builds with every passing minute, and every beep says that the 7.30 bookings are walking through the door and being seated. The careful arrangement of arrival times has now been largely wasted. Incidents such as these are what annoy Philippa and Donovan the most, not because they think it's rude, but because it will throw the kitchen into chaos and standards may start to fall. 'It means we can't perform at our best for everyone, and our best is what people expect and what they deserve. If one table is late it means that everyone has to wait that bit longer – it's not like we're just slinging a few extra hamburgers onto a hot plate. There are no shortcuts with food like ours.' **7.35 p.m.** Joseph is having trouble keeping up with the appetisers. Donovan needs him elsewhere. 'C'mon Jethro, how long does it take to do four bloody soups? Get on to that trout now.' **7.45 p.m.** Members of the large group have all finally arrived, thirty minutes after their booking time. The 8 o'clock time slot is now looking like it could get out of control. The kitchen is in full swing. Bodies fly about and all verbal communication is reduced to the strictly necessary: 'hot behind', 'mind your head', 'how long on the pithivier?' Donovan seems to know what everyone is up to and is keeping a particular eye on Joseph. 'He needs one good bollocking for the evening and then he's right. Don't you, Jethro?' Joseph nods, not missing a beat. Philippa is still overseeing the dressing of the plates, tasting and refining as she goes. **8.00 p.m.** Either the door has been propped open or all of the 8 o'clock bookings have arrived at once. It's the latter. Donovan: 'This is where it starts getting messy.' In the next fifteen minutes twenty-two people will be placing their orders and to make matters worse, the docket from the large group has only just reached the kitchen. The first of the desserts go out. **8.20 p.m.** The door buzzer is still going and the dockets on the board are lining up at an alarming rate. Despite having copped a hot pan on top of his hand Donovan is deftly boning the pigeons he's just poached. Ben dresses the plate with ravioli and cabbage in readiness. Somehow Donovan still manages to know what is going on in every corner of the kitchen. He notices that there are too many dockets for them to keep up with and tells Josephine to let the waiters know not to take any more for a while – people should not have to wait too long after they've ordered. Another six tables – fourteen people – are due in at 8.30. **8.30 p.m.** Desserts, entrées and mains are crossing at the pass. Philippa stops a pigeon en vessie going out without its accompanying consommé. The pace in the kitchen seems to be getting faster although it doesn't seem humanly possible. 'Hot behind' is now 'hind'. Philippa is the one oasis of calm in the room: her economy of movement and steadiness of hand means she gets a lot done with the minimum of fuss; she's fast, she doesn't get in anyone's way, and she only has to do things once. Donovan: 'Josephine take that order out of your pocket. If it's been taken I need to know it's there. And tell 'em again, no more orders.' The door keeps beeping, announcing six more tables. **8.35 p.m.** Disaster. Front of house has oversold the hare pithivier so Philippa's in the cold larder assemb-ling one, which means there's one less person to dress the plates. Now that has to be done solely by the same people who are cooking. They all have to work even faster, but the plates still have to be perfect on the way out – another thing for Donovan to keep his eye on now. 'Thought you'd sneak that past me, Jethro? You shithead.' And then, 'Service. Now. Come on. Hot food.' Sending out food that is imperfectly presented, even if the faults would not be apparent to the uninitiated, is the very worst thing you can do in this kitchen. It's the one thing that's sure to incur Donovan's and Philippa's wrath. **8.40 p.m.** Appetisers go out amidst the mains, entrées and desserts, which are the only serene, ordered-looking things in sight. The already well-covered pin board takes another few dockets. A request arrives from a diner: it would mean a lot to him if he could have some soup to take home, he enjoyed it so much. Of course he can, but Donovan doesn't have time to enjoy the compliment – 'Take care of that, Jethro'. Joseph looks up from the plates he's dressing with a 'does not compute' expression, finishes with the plate and starts searching for something to put the soup in. 'He's not leaving now, Jethro. Three dory – start dressing. Jesus, mate.' **8.55 p.m.** Things are still going at a cracking pace and it's hard to believe that they can continue to keep up. A plate comes back that still has a lot of food on it. Amidst the chaos Donovan spots it, 'What was wrong with that trotter?' Josephine assures him that the lady was very complimentary but did not have a very big appetite. He seems satisfied with the answer. He turns, slides a pan into the oven and slams the door. **9.20 p.m.** Philippa is in the cold larder with Karen; the focus of the action is starting to change as the tiny area is deluged with dessert orders. The small section formerly used for cold entrées is reclaimed for desserts. Philippa: 'Jethro, clean this trout crap away. I need the space. Now!' Every now and again she darts back to help with the mains and the odd entrée still going out. The kitchen hands are only just managing to keep up with the demand. Fiona, balancing a tower of pans, manages to make it from one side of the kitchen to the other without bumping into anybody or losing her footing on the now slippery floor. **10.30 p.m.** All of a sudden the worst of it is over, although the cold larder is busy. Josh and Ben talk about the night's service. Everyone is chewing on leftover bread rolls and Brussels sprouts purée. Karen and Philippa are still in the cold larder assembling desserts. **10.45 p.m.** The last of the desserts leaves the kitchen. The kitchen hands are ploughing through the piles of pans and dishes. Donovan looks exhausted. 'I thought we were gonna lose it there for a while. I might even have a beer tonight.' The stove is turned down and the veal stock goes on for tomorrow. Jenny George

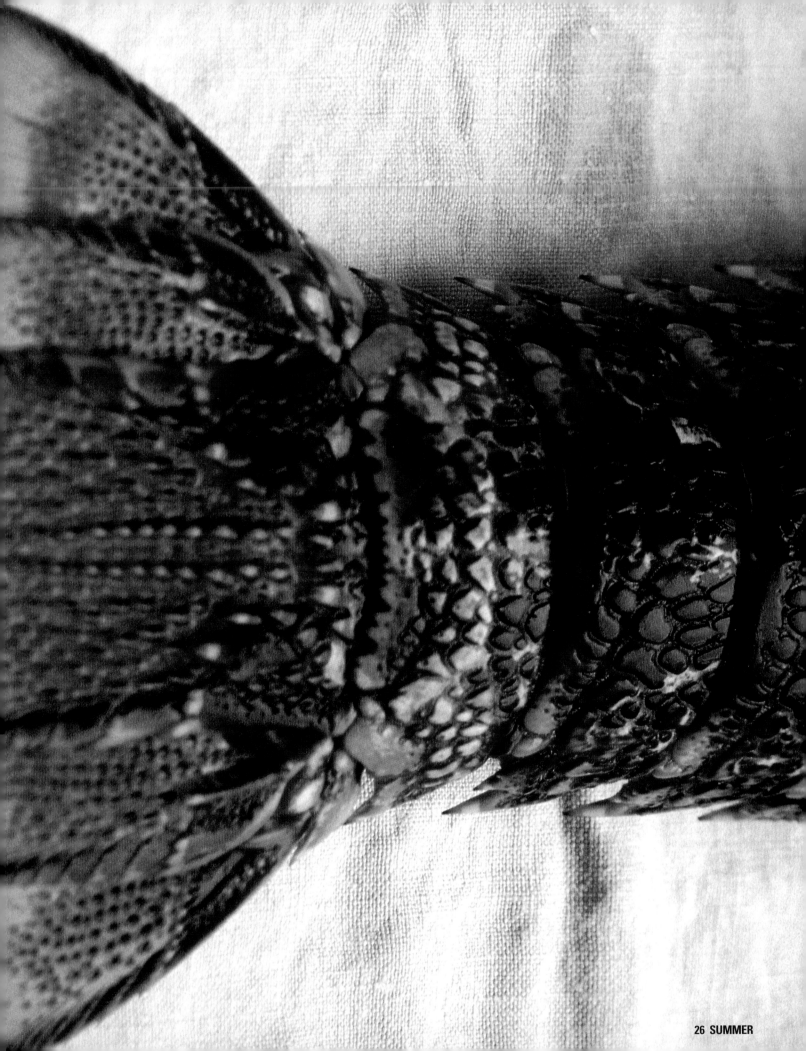

The essence of summer in a bowl — the pleasure of vine-ripened tomatoes is captured in this fragrant emulsion of vegetable juices and virgin olive oil. The sweet crab and smooth avocado make each mouthful a revelation.

2kg (4½ lb) ripe tomatoes, chopped
2 red capsicum, chopped
1 cucumber, chopped
2 onions, chopped
2 cloves garlic, chopped
240g (8½ oz) stale white bread, diced
4 egg yolks
3 tablespoons olive oil
2 tablespoons red wine vinegar
1 cucumber
lemon juice

Avocado Mousse
2 avocados
juice of 1 lime
1 leaf gelatine, softened in some cold water

Tian
2 red capsicum
2 blue swimmer crabs
6 leaves basil, finely julienned
2 tablespoons Mayonnaise (page 152)

Put the tomatoes, capsicum, cucumber, onions and garlic into a liquidiser and blitz for 2 to 5 minutes. Soak the bread in the puréed vegetables for 3 hours. The bread gives the soup some body and texture.

For the mousse, put 1½ avocados into a food processor and blend until smooth. Cut the remaining avocado into small dice and fold through. Bring the lime juice to the boil then add the gelatine. Fold into the avocado, season with salt and pepper and pour into a bowl. Allow to set in the fridge for at least 1 hour.

For the tian, first grill the capsicum in some olive oil until the skin blisters. When cool peel off the skin and discard the seeds. Chop the flesh into small dice. Remove all the meat from the crabs while still raw. (The easiest way is with scissors and a toothpick.) Sort through to check that there is no shell or cartilage remaining. Sauté the crab meat in a little olive oil. Drain and allow to cool. To this add the capsicum, then the basil. Mix well together, bind with the mayonnaise and season with salt and pepper.

Strain the soup, pressing down on the sieve to push through some of the solids. Put the egg yolks into a bowl and whisk in the soup. Gradually add the olive oil and whisk until it emulsifies. Add the red wine vinegar and then season.

Peel the cucumber and slice thinly lengthwise. Cut into long julienne and toss with some lemon juice. Season with salt and pepper. To serve, place a quenelle of the avocado mousse in a serving bowl. Arrange a mound of crab next to this and a ball of cucumber spaghetti. Pour in the cold soup.

Serves 4

GAZPACHO WITH TIAN OF CRAB, CUCUMBER SPAGHETTI AND AVOCADO MOUSSE

A beautiful combination of earth, sun and sea, this dish is a tribute to summer vegetables in their prime.

2 x 500g (1 lb 2 oz) crayfish
4 Kipfler potatoes, whole
100ml (3½ fl oz) extra-virgin olive oil
1 tablespoon white wine vinegar
1 clove garlic, chopped
1 sprig thyme, chopped
1 bay leaf, chopped
200g (7 oz) green beans, topped and tailed
4 ripe tomatoes
2 shallots, chopped
1 truffle, sliced

Court-bouillon
1 carrot, chopped
1 onion, chopped
1 stick celery, chopped
1 head garlic, halved across
1 bay leaf, chopped
1 sprig thyme, chopped
50ml (1¾ fl oz) white wine
3 litres (6 pints) water

For the court-bouillon, bring all the ingredients to the boil and boil for 2 to 5 minutes.

Plunge the crayfish in the boiling court-bouillon. Remove from the heat and allow to cool. When cool, shell the tails and extract the meat from the head and legs.

Cook the potatoes in salted water in their skins.

Make a vinaigrette by whisking together the olive oil, vinegar, garlic, thyme and bay leaf. When the potatoes are cooked, peel and place in the vinaigrette so they absorb the flavours.

Blanch the green beans in boiling salted water, then refresh in ice water. Split the beans in half lengthwise, then halve again and cut into fine julienne.

Blanch and peel the tomatoes and cut in half. Cook in the oven at 80°C (175°F/Gas mark ¼) for 2 hours with a little olive oil splashed on them.

To serve, cut the potatoes into rounds and arrange in the centre of the plate. Cut the crayfish into 2cm (¾ in) medallions. Arrange the crayfish on top of the potatoes. Season. Dress the beans with a little of the vinaigrette, add the shallots and season with salt and pepper. Place the beans on top of the crayfish, then top with the tomato and sliced truffle.

Serves 4

SALAD OF KING ISLAND CRAYFISH, MARINATED POTATOES, GREEN BEANS, CONFIT TOMATOES AND TRUFFLE

The sweetness of the apple and acidity of tomato, teamed with the velvety bavarois, make for clean and refreshing flavours on the palate.

36 large yabbies
12 ripe Roma tomatoes
2 pinches sea salt
2 pinches caster sugar
50ml (1¾ fl oz) olive oil
1 sprig thyme, chopped
1 clove garlic, chopped
6 sticks celery, peeled and cut into fine julienne
2 Golden Delicious apples, peeled, cored and finely diced
juice of 1 lemon
1 shallot, chopped

Fennel Bavarois
3 shallots, finely chopped
3 bulbs fennel, finely chopped
300ml (½ pint) Vegetable Nage (page 152)
300ml (½ pint) thickened cream
2 leaves gelatine, soaked in cold water
2 tablespoons chopped dill

Sauté the yabbies in hot vegetable oil until the shells turn red. Shell.

Preheat the oven to 80°C (175°F/Gas mark ¼).

Blanch and peel the tomatoes, then seed them. Sprinkle with sea salt and sugar, then drizzle with olive oil. Add the thyme and garlic, then place in the oven for 2 hours. Check after 1½ hours. Do not let the tomatoes dry out, they must remain soft and moist. Chop coarsely and store in the olive oil.

For the fennel bavarois, sweat the shallots in olive oil without colouring for around 5 minutes or until cooked, then add the fennel. Cover and cook for 5 minutes or until the fennel is tender. Add the nage and reduce by two-thirds, then add the cream and boil for around 10 minutes. Liquidise and pass through a fine strainer. You should have 550ml (1 pint/2¼ cups) of fennel mixture (if not add more cream to make up this amount). Add the gelatine leaves to the hot mixture, stir, strain and season. Add the dill. Pour into 6.5cm (2½in) moulds and chill for around 4 hours.

Unmould the bavarois by dipping the mould into hot water. (They should be served at room temperature.) Place the bavarois on the serving plate.

Submerge the celery in ice water for 2 minutes to curl and crisp it. Drain, then season with some of the tomato oil and lemon juice.

Mix the diced apples and tomatoes, season and place the mixture into a 6cm (2½in) pastry cutter on the plate beside the bavarois.

Toss the yabbies in the oil from the tomatoes, season and place on top of the apple mix. Place the celery on top of the yabbies, then carefully remove the cutter.

Serves 4

ROASTED YABBY TAILS, APPLE, CELERY AND CONFIT TOMATO SALAD, FENNEL BAVAROIS

At est est est this dish has surfaced in many different guises – we have substituted both yabby and crab for the crayfish, and in place of the herb salad, we sometimes serve a tangle of crisp, sliced fennel.

1 small salmon fillet
1 quantity Court-bouillon (page 32)
1 x 500g (1lb 2oz) crayfish
8 Kipfler potatoes, whole
1 bunch tarragon
80ml (2¾ fl oz) Shellfish Oil (page 152)
juice of 1 lemon
mâche, frisée, rocket, chervil pluches
chives, cut into batons
witlof, cut into julienne

Sauce
1 carrot, finely chopped
½ onion, finely chopped
1 stick celery, finely chopped
4 cloves garlic, finely chopped
250ml (9 fl oz/1 cup) Veal Stock (page 152)
250ml (9 fl oz/1 cup) Fish Stock (page 152)
tarragon stalks
50g (1¾ oz) butter
50ml (1¾ fl oz) cream

Skin the salmon and cut into a pavé, a thin tile around 1cm (½in) thick.

Prepare the bouillon according to the instructions on page 32, bring to the boil and blanch the crayfish for approximately 30 seconds. Remove the head and shell (reserve for the stock), extract the meat from the tail and chop roughly.

Boil the potatoes in their skins until cooked. Peel and set aside.

Pick the tarragon, keeping all the small leaves for the salad, the larger leaves for the potatoes and the stalks for the sauce.

For the sauce, chop the reserved shell and head into small pieces. Sauté in hot vegetable oil until golden (be careful not to over-brown or the stock will be bitter). Add the carrot, onion, celery and garlic, sweat without colouring. Cover with the stocks and bring to the boil. Add the tarragon stalks, cook rapidly for 30 minutes, and strain. Reduce by half then add the butter and cream. Keep warm.

Reheat the potatoes in hot water.

Put two-thirds of the shellfish oil in a pan, add the tarragon leaves and the crayfish meat and heat gently. Add the potatoes and crush with a fork. Season with salt and pepper and add some lemon juice.

Sear the salmon in a very hot pan, keeping it very rare. Dress the salad greens with the remaining shellfish oil and a squeeze of lemon juice. Put the potatoes in the centre of a plate, place the salmon on top, then the salad. Drizzle the sauce around.

Serves 4

PAVE OF ATLANTIC SALMON, CRUSHED KIPFLER POTATOES WITH CRAYFISH AND TARRAGON, HERB SALAD

A delicious entrée or light main course inspired by the classical accompaniments to caviar. The intense sea-salty caviar, mild freshwater fish and crunchy celery provide lots of interest in the mouth.

4 x 450-500g (1–1lb 2 oz) silver perch
1 head celery
4 eggs, hardboiled and refreshed
1 lemon, segmented
4 shallots, finely chopped
8 cornichons, sliced into rounds
2 tablespoons baby capers, whole
2 tablespoons chopped parsley

Remoulade
80ml (2¾ fl oz) Mayonnaise (page 152)
juice of 1 lemon
50ml (1¾ fl oz) Fish Stock (page 152), reduced by half
40ml (1½ fl oz) whipped cream
100g (3½ oz) Osietra caviar

Fillet and scale the fish, and remove all the pin bones with a pair of tweezers. Wash and set aside.

String the celery and slice stalks diagonally on an angle.

Shell the eggs, separating the yolks and whites. Peel and segment the lemon, then dice the flesh finely.

For the remoulade, add the mayonnaise and lemon juice to the reduced fish stock, then fold in the whipped cream. Season. Just before serving add the caviar. (If you add the caviar too early the lemon juice will cook it.)

Pan-fry the fish in olive oil, skin-side down, until the skin is crispy. Sauté the celery in hot olive oil until crisp. Season.

To serve, scatter the chopped egg and the shallots, cornichons, capers, parsley and lemon around the edge of the plate. Spoon a circle of remoulade into the centre, top with the celery and stack on the fish.

Serves 4

SILVER PERCH, OSIETRA CAVIAR REMOULADE AND CRISPY CELERY, 'CLASSIC CAVIAR GARNISH'

A refined version of a peasant dish. The robust flavours and colours of the rock fish and saffron consommé bind the dish together beautifully.

2 red mullet, 2 John Dory, 12 scallops, 8 mussels, 8 clams, 8 prawns
a little white wine, 1 bunch tarragon
4 tomatoes, peeled, seeded and diced
2 bulbs fennel, sliced
50ml (1¾ fl oz) olive oil
150ml (5 fl oz) Fish Stock (page 152)

Consommé
6 red mullet
1 carrot, 1 leek, 2 sticks celery and 1 onion, all chopped
tarragon stalks, 1 bay leaf, 1 sprig thyme
4 tomatoes, chopped into 1cm (½ in) dice
2 tablespoons tomato paste, 2 pinches saffron
50ml (1¾ fl oz) cognac
50ml (1¾ fl oz) Ricard
50ml (1¾ fl oz) white wine
2 litres (4 pints) Fish Stock (page 152)
8 egg whites

Tortellini
1 egg white, 40ml (1½ fl oz) cream
1 pinch saffron
20ml (¾ fl oz) Fish Stock (page 152)
150g (5 oz) Pasta (page 154)

Fillet the red mullet and the John Dory, trim and remove the pin bones. Reserve the trimmings for the clarification. Clean the scallops, removing the roe. Cook the mussels and clams in a little white wine until they open. Reserve the liquor for the consommé. Pick the small leaves of tarragon.

For the consommé, cut the 6 mullet and bones into 2cm (¾ in) pieces, making sure all the guts and gills are removed. Rinse and pat dry. Sauté all the bones and trimmings in hot vegetable oil until golden (do not over-colour or the consommé will become bitter). In a separate pan, sweat the carrot, leek, celery, onion and the fennel trimmings in vegetable oil without colouring. Add the herbs, tomatoes, tomato paste and saffron. Deglaze with cognac, reduce to a glaze. Add the Ricard and white wine and reduce again. Cover with the fish stock, bring to the boil, add the fish and bones, and cook this stock for 1 hour. Add the mussel and clam juices just before straining. Strain this stock and allow to cool completely.

Blend the reserved fish trimmings in a food processor with the egg whites. Whisk this into the chilled stock, then place on the heat and continue whisking until it comes to the boil. Reduce heat and simmer gently for 30 minutes. The whites will form a raft. When the stock is clear, strain through muslin.

For the tortellini, take 4 of the prawns and blend in a food processor, then add the egg white and cream. Put the saffron in a pan and heat slightly, then add the fish stock to extract all the flavour from the saffron. Add this to the prawn mixture and mix through.

Roll out the pasta into a thin sheet and cut into rounds using a 4cm (1½in) pastry cutter. Place 1 teaspoon filling on the bottom half of the pasta round, and fold down the top to make a semi-circle. Press to seal the edge, then twist the 2 ends together to form a tortellini. Repeat with the rest of the pasta and filling.

Pan-fry the red mullet, John Dory and prawns in a hot pan in olive oil for 2 to 3 minutes. Add the scallops. Do not overcook.

Cook the fennel in an emulsion of olive oil and fish stock until just crisp. Cook the tortellini in boiling water for 2 to 3 minutes.

To serve, scatter the fennel at the bottom of a serving dish with the tomato dice. Arrange the fish on top. Add the tortellini and top with the small tarragon leaves. Pour the hot consommé over the top.

Serves 4

BOUILLABAISSE OF ROCK FISH, CROQUANT OF FENNEL, TARRAGON AND SAFFRON TORTELLINI

Poaching in a bag intensifies the flavour of the truffle and keeps the bird perfectly moist and succulent. A luxurious dish, perfect for the festive season.

2 free-range chicken barrels
2 truffles, thinly sliced
500g (1 lb 2 oz) Pasta (page 154)
2 bunches asparagus, trimmed
2 bunches baby leeks, trimmed
20ml (3/4 fl oz) olive oil
50ml (1 3/4 fl oz) Chicken Stock (page 152)

Sauce

1kg (2 1/4 lb) chicken wings,
    chopped into 1cm (1/2 in) pieces
2 shallots, finely chopped
1 leek, finely chopped
1 stick celery, finely chopped
375ml (13 fl oz/1 1/2 cups) champagne
2 litres (4 pints) Chicken Stock (page 152)
1 head garlic, halved across
150ml (5 fl oz) cream

Remove the winglets and wishbones from the chicken. Put some vegetable oil on your hands and slowly work your fingers under the skin. Start from the neck end, taking care not to tear the skin.

Oil and season the truffle slices with olive oil, then place them between the skin and flesh on either side of the breasts. Season the chicken inside and out with salt and pepper. Place a kitchen bag into another to create a double-layered bag. Inside each double-layered bag place 1 chicken. Expel all the air from the bags and tie the top tightly with string. (If you do not expel all the air, the bag will float when you put it in simmering water.)

For the sauce, blanch the wings and rinse. Sweat the shallots, leek and celery in some vegetable oil without colouring. Add the chicken wings. Deglaze with two-thirds of the champagne. Reduce by half, then cover with the chicken stock. Bring to the boil and cook for 1 hour, then add the garlic. Strain and reduce by half. Whisk in the cream, season and add the remaining champagne.

Roll the pasta through the thinnest setting of the pasta machine and cut into fine noodles. Blanch in boiling water for 30 seconds then refresh in ice water.

Cook the chicken in a deep pan of water at 80°C (175°F) for 30 minutes, then rest for 15 minutes. (You can cook the chicken ahead to this point.)

To reheat, submerge the chickens for 2 to 3 minutes in hot water. Remove them from the bags and take the breasts off the bone.

Cook the asparagus and leek in the olive oil and chicken stock until tender. Reheat the pasta by blanching in hot water.

To serve, roll the pasta into a ball, top with the leeks and asparagus. Place the chicken on the plate and spoon over sauce.

Serves 4

CHICKEN WITH TRUFFLES AND CHAMPAGNE 'EN VESSIE', FRESH NOODLES, ASPARAGUS AND LEEKS

The combination of cinnamon and rabbit is a flavour triumph. The lemon dust is also delicious stirred into a risotto or sprinkled on seafood.

4 rabbit shoulders
½ cinnamon stick, crushed
grated zest of 1 lemon
50g (1¾ oz) rock salt
150ml (5 fl oz) duck fat
3 lemons
200g (7 oz) Pasta (page 154)
4 rabbit saddles
1 stick celery, cut into ribbons
4 carrots, cut into ribbons
4 leeks, cut into ribbons
4 heads witlof, cut into ribbons
50ml (1¾ fl oz) Chicken Stock (page 152)

Sauce

1kg (2¼ lb) rabbit bones, chopped into small pieces
1 leek, finely diced
1 onion, finely diced
2 sticks celery, finely diced
2 heads garlic, halved across
1 bay leaf
1 sprig thyme
3 litres (6 pints) Chicken Stock (page 152)
1½ cinnamon sticks
zest and juice of 2 lemons
100ml (3½ fl oz) thickened cream
50g (1¾ oz) butter

Trim the rabbit shoulders, removing any excess fat. Combine cinnamon and lemon zest with the rock salt. When well mixed, scatter it over the rabbit shoulders and let stand for 4 hours.

Preheat the oven to 80°C (175°F/Gas mark ¼). Scrape off the salt and rinse quickly. Melt the duck fat and submerge the shoulders. Cook in the oven for around 3 hours. Allow to sit until cool.

For the sauce, blanch the bones in boiling water, then rinse. Sweat the leek, onion, celery and garlic in vegetable oil in a pot without colouring. Add the bay leaf and thyme. Add the bones and cover with chicken stock. Bring to the boil, then add 1 cinnamon stick and zest of 1 lemon. Simmer for 1 hour then strain. Reduce the stock to two-thirds with the remaining cinnamon and zest. Whisk in the cream and butter and finish with the lemon juice, salt and pepper.

For the lemon dust, peel the lemons and remove all white pith. Place the skins on a baking tray and dry in an 80°C (175°F/Gas mark ¼) oven for 2 hours. When totally dry, grind in a spice grinder to a fine powder.

Roll out the pasta through the thinnest setting of your machine and cut into fine tagliatelle. Blanch in rapidly boiling water, then refresh in ice water. When totally cold, strain, then drizzle over the olive oil. Set aside.

Preheat the oven to 260°C (500°F/Gas mark 9). Roast the saddles for 6 to 8 minutes, depending on their size. Allow to rest for around 5 minutes. Take the saddle off the bone and carve.

Drizzle a little olive oil into a frying pan, heat and add the vegetables. Toss for 20 seconds, then add the chicken stock and allow to boil rapidly until all the liquid has gone. (Cooking vegetables like this glazes them and intensifies their colour and flavour.) Season with salt and pepper.

Reheat the pasta in some boiling water. Reheat the shoulder in the duck fat and take the meat off the bone.

To serve, place a mound of vegetable ribbons on the serving plate. Place the saddle on top. Roll the pasta into a ball and place on the plate. Place the shredded shoulder on top and garnish with lemon dust. Spoon over the sauce.

Serves 4

ROASTED SADDLE OF RABBIT, CONFIT SHOULDER, FRESH NOODLES, CINNAMON AND LEMON SAUCE

A dessert that shows off jewel-coloured berries in their prime. It tastes as good as it looks – the berries' sweetness is tempered by the tangy sorbet.

1 punnet each of:
raspberries
blueberries
loganberries
redcurrants
wild strawberries
strawberries, sliced

Strawberry Juice
1kg (2 1/4 lb) large red strawberries, sliced
120g (4 1/4 oz) caster sugar

Yoghurt Sorbet
700ml (1 1/4 pints) milk
300g (10 1/2 oz) caster sugar
150ml (5 fl oz) liquid glucose
1 litre (2 pints / 4 cups) yoghurt
juice of 2 lemons

For the strawberry juice, put the strawberries and sugar in a stainless steel bowl and mix gently. Leave in a warm place for 1 hour and refrigerate overnight. Strain through a fine sieve lined with muslin, then chill until required.

For the yoghurt sorbet, bring the milk to the boil with the sugar and glucose, and cool completely. Whisk into the yoghurt, add the lemon juice and refrigerate until 2 to 3 hours before needed. Churn in an ice-cream machine according to the manufacturer's instructions and freeze. (If churned too early the sorbet will become too hard.)

To serve, scatter the berries around the serving bowls. Place some strawberries in the middle and a generous scoop of sorbet on top. Pour in some strawberry juice and serve.

Serves 4

CHILLED STRAWBERRY SOUP WITH SUMMER BERRIES AND YOGHURT SORBET

It's worth the extra effort of cutting out the sablé into star shapes – your guests will be amused by the association!

½ quantity Sablé (page 154)
1 quantity Apricot Sorbet (page 156)
Confit Zest (page 156)

Star Anise Mousse
6 egg yolks
140g (5 oz) caster sugar
1 tablespoon water
70ml (2½ fl oz) Pastis or Ricard
juice of 1 lemon
1½ leaves gelatine, soaked in water
450ml (16 fl oz) lightly whipped cream

Poaching Liquid
1 litre (2 pints/4 cups) water
500g (1 lb 2 oz) caster sugar
375ml (13 fl oz/1½ cups) sweet white wine (sauternes)
1 vanilla bean
2 star anise pods
juice of 1 lemon
18 apricot halves

Preheat the oven to 160°C (325°F/Gas mark 3).

Bring pastry out of the fridge and place in a cool place an hour before using to soften slightly.

Cut out 5mm (¼ in) slices of pastry. Roll the disks out to about 3mm (⅛ in) and cut into desired shapes. (They will be extremely delicate.) Place on baking paper, well spaced, and bake in the oven for 10 minutes or until the pastry is just golden around the edges.

For the star anise mousse, line a 20cm x 15cm (8 in x 6 in) tray with baking paper. Put the egg yolks in the bowl of an electric mixer. In a small saucepan, bring the sugar and water to the boil and when the temperature reaches 115°C (239°F) start whisking the egg yolks. Once the sugar reaches 118°C (244°F) remove from the heat and pour in a steady stream down the side of the bowl onto the whisking egg yolks. Continue beating until cold.

Heat the Pastis and lemon juice in a saucepan and swirl in the gelatine. Add to this a third of the yolk mixture, then fold into the rest. Fold in the cream, taking care not to overmix. Spread into the tray and freeze until 30 minutes before needed.

For the poaching liquid, bring all the ingredients to the boil except the apricots. Reduce to a simmer, add the fruit and cook gently for 5 minutes. Allow to cool in the liquid. Gently remove the apricots from the liquid. For the sauce reduce 250ml (9 fl oz/1 cup) poaching liquid to 125ml (4 fl oz/½ cup).

Prepare the apricot sorbet according to the instructions on page 156.

To serve, put a sablé biscuit in the middle of each plate. Using a cutter slightly smaller than the biscuit, cut out a disc of mousse and place on top. Top with another biscuit, then, using a piping bag, pipe a circle of sorbet on top. Dust another biscuit with icing sugar and place on top of the sorbet. Place 3 poached apricot halves around the plate with some lemon confit. Drizzle some sauce around and serve.

Serves 4

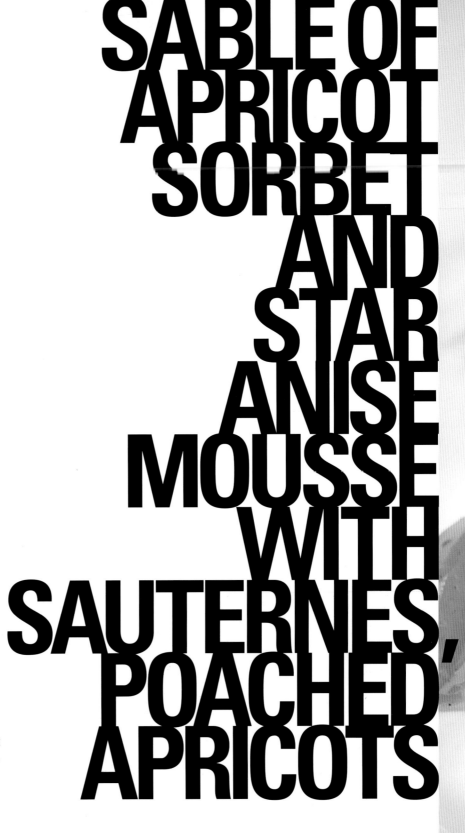

SABLE OF APRICOT SORBET AND STAR ANISE MOUSSE WITH SAUTERNES, POACHED APRICOTS

An adult version of a nursery favourite. You can make the trifle in a large dish instead of parfait glasses.

1 quantity Biscuit Joconde (page 154)
3 punnets fresh blackberries
1 quantity Lemon Cream (page 112)
1 quantity Green Apple Sorbet (page 156)
1 Granny Smith apple, diced

Blackberry Jelly
1kg (2 1/4 lb) frozen blackberries
150g (5 oz) caster sugar
20ml (3/4 fl oz) kirsch
2 leaves gelatine, soaked in cold water

Vanilla Cream
500ml (18 fl oz / 2 cups) cream
1 vanilla bean
95g (3 1/2 oz) caster sugar
6 egg yolks
1/2 leaf gelatine, soaked in cold water

For the blackberry jelly, thaw the frozen blackberries in a warm place. Strain off the juice – you should have about 400ml (14 fl oz). In a stainless steel saucepan heat the juice with the sugar and the kirsch until the sugar is dissolved. Swirl in the gelatine. Allow to cool but do not refrigerate.

For the vanilla cream, bring the cream and vanilla bean to the boil. Whisk the sugar into the egg yolks until pale and thick. Whisk in the cream and return to the pan. Cook over moderate heat until the mixture coats the back of a spoon. Stir in the gelatine, strain and allow to cool. Refrigerate.

Cut the biscuit joconde into discs slightly smaller than the diameter of your serving dish or parfait glass.

To assemble, place about 5 to 6 blackberries in the bottom of the parfait glasses. Carefully spoon over a little of the blackberry jelly, just enough to barely cover. Refrigerate until set.

Place the lemon cream in a piping bag and gently pipe a layer over the jelly. Then place a disk of biscuit joconde, followed by a generous spoonful of vanilla cream, biscuit, blackberries and jelly. Refrigerate to set the jelly.

Pipe another layer of lemon cream and top with a layer of jelly nearly to the rim of the glass. Refrigerate until ready to serve.

To serve, place a trifle on one side of the plate and a scoop of sorbet on the diced apple.

Serves 6

FRESH BLACK- BERRY AND LEMON CREAM TRIFLE WITH GREEN APPLE SORBET

Mid-to late-summer brings together two of our favourite flavours: perfect yellow peaches and lemon verbena. Make the most of them – and plant some lemon verbena if you have the space.

1 quantity Pâte Sucrée (page 154)

Peaches
600g (1 lb 5 oz) caster sugar
2 litres (4 pints) water
1 vanilla bean
6 perfect yellow peaches

Mascarpone Filling
zest of 1 lime
110g (4 oz) caster sugar
250ml (9 fl oz) cream
10 fresh lemon verbena leaves
5 egg yolks
1 egg white
250g (9 oz) mascarpone

You will need 6 7.5cm (3 in) dessert rings or a 22cm (8½ in) tart ring for this. To poach the peaches, bring the sugar, water and vanilla bean to the boil for 10 minutes. Reduce the heat. Skin peaches by plunging them into a pan of boiling water and then into ice water. The skin should slip straight off. Place the peaches in the syrup and turn the heat back up. Once the syrup comes back to the boil turn down the heat to a simmer and poach for approximately 10 minutes. Allow the peaches to cool in the syrup.

For the mascarpone filling, rub the lime zest through the sugar. Bring the cream to the boil, add the verbena (crush the leaves slightly in your hands) and sugar and stir to dissolve. Infuse for 10 minutes. Warm again slightly.

Whisk the egg yolks and white and add to the cream mixture. Strain onto the mascarpone and whisk until very smooth.

Prepare the pastry according to the instructions on page 154 and roll out to a thickness of 3mm (⅛ in). Carefully line the tart ring or rings, making sure there are no creases or the filling will leak. Allow the pastry to hang over the ring – this will be trimmed off after filling and cooling. Refrigerate for 30 minutes, then line with foil and fill with rice.

Preheat the oven to 180°C (350°F/Gas mark 4).

Blind bake the pastry shell: about 30 minutes for the large tin and 20 minutes for the small ones. Remove the foil and rice and continue baking until the pastry is golden brown all over.

Reduce the oven to 140°C (275°F/Gas mark 1). Fill the shells with the mascarpone mix and bake for about 40 minutes for a large tart or 25 minutes for the small. They should wobble without being liquid. Once they are completely cool, trim off the pastry overhang.

For the sauce reduce 200ml (7 fl oz) of the poaching liquid by half.

To serve, dust the tart or tartlets with icing sugar; slice the large tart into wedges. Place a peach on a serving plate, and a wedge of tart or a tartlet by the side. Spoon some sauce around the peach and serve.

Serves 6

POACHED YELLOW PEACHES WITH A LEMON VERBENA-SCENTED MASCARPONE TART

STEP BY STEP PYRAMID OF STRAWBERRY SORBET AND PINK CHAMPAGNE PARFAIT WITH A SALAD OF MELONS AND WILD STRAW-BERRIES

A dish inspired by the affinity of strawberries with champagne. To simplify this dish, omit the gelatine from the parfait and churn as an ice-cream. Serve with the melons and strawberries.

½ quantity Strawberry Sorbet (page 156)
honeydew
cantaloupe
champagne melon
watermelon
wild strawberries (fraises des bois)
200ml (7 fl oz) Strawberry Juice (page 46)

Champagne Parfait
110g (4 oz) egg yolks
125ml (4 fl oz /½ cup) Sugar Syrup (page 156)
20ml (¾ fl oz) lemon juice
2 leaves gelatine, soaked in cold water
180ml (6½ fl oz) pink champagne, chilled
250ml (9 fl oz /1 cup) lightly whipped cream

Nougatine
250g (9 oz) fondant
30g (1 oz) flaked almonds, lightly toasted

Serves 4

LINE
PYRAMIDS
FILL
MOULDS

Make the strawberry sorbet according to the instructions on page 156, churn and freeze. Using a palette knife, spread some sorbet onto each panel of the mould. Refreeze.

For the champagne parfait, put the egg yolks in the bowl of an electric mixer. Bring the sugar syrup to 110°C (225°F) then start whisking the eggs. When the syrup reaches 121°C (250°F) pour into the yolks in a thin stream, whisking all the time. Continue whisking until cold.

Heat the lemon juice and swirl in the gelatine leaves, making sure they dissolve completely. Mix a little of the sabayon (yolk mixture) with the gelatine, then mix in the rest. Pour in the champagne and fold in very quickly with a whisk. Fold in the cream. Pour into the moulds and freeze. Preheat the oven to 180°C (350°F/Gas mark 4).

For the nougatine, caramelise the fondant until pale golden in a heavy-based saucepan. Spread the almonds on a tray lined with baking paper. Pour on the fondant and allow to cool completely, then pulverise in a food processor. To make the triangles, sift a thin layer of the powder onto the back of a very lightly oiled baking tray. Place in the oven until melted. Allow to cool slightly then, using a pyramid stencil, cut out the shapes. If the nougatine becomes too hard to work with, return to the oven to soften. Remove the triangles from the tray and flatten with the palm of your hand. Store in an airtight tin until ready to use.

Scoop out the melon flesh using a baller. Hull the fraises des bois.

To serve, put a knife in the centre of the pyramid and run the mould under hot water briefly. Gently ease out and place in the middle of a serving plate. Lean the nougatine pyramids against each side of the pyramid. Surround with melon balls and fraises des bois. Spoon the strawberry juice around and serve immediately.

DUST
TRAY
CUT
TRIANGLES

AUTUMN

Crisp pastry, herby crêpes, slippery mushrooms and truffle-flavoured mousse. The layered colours and earthy aromas combine to make this a quintessentially autumn dish.

12 large slippery jacks
8 medium-sized pine mushrooms
4 tablespoons Chicken Mousse (page 152)
1 bunch chives, finely chopped
1 teaspoon chopped truffle (optional)
1 tablespoon truffle oil
4 Herb Pancakes (page 152)
500g (1 lb 2 oz) Puff Pastry (page 154)
egg yolk

Sauce
1kg (2¼ lb) chicken wings, chopped into small pieces
10 shallots, sliced
200g (7 oz) button mushrooms, sliced
1 head garlic, roughly chopped
1 tablespoon sherry vinegar
375ml (13 fl oz/1½ cups) Madeira
1 litre (2 pints/4 cups) Veal Stock (page 152)
1 litre (2 pints/4 cups) Chicken Stock (page 152)
1 bay leaf
1 sprig thyme
2 tablespoons cream
50g (1¾ oz) butter

Trim the stalks from the slippery jacks and pine mushrooms. Dice the pine mushrooms. Sauté the slippery jacks in hot olive oil until tender, then cool on kitchen paper. Sauté the pine mushrooms in hot olive oil and cool on kitchen paper.

Fold the pine mushrooms through the chicken mousse, add the chives, truffle and truffle oil. Season with salt and pepper, and refrigerate until needed.

Prepare the pancakes as on page 152. On each pancake smear some mousse, then top with a slippery jack, then more mousse and another slippery jack. Repeat. Fold the pancake around the filling to make a neat round parcel. Refrigerate the parcels while you make the sauce.

For the sauce, sauté the chicken wings in hot vegetable oil until golden brown. Drain the wings in a colander. Sweat the shallots and mushrooms in some vegetable oil in a heavy-based saucepan, add the garlic and allow to colour slightly. Deglaze the pan with sherry vinegar, add the Madeira and reduce by half. Add the chicken wings, stocks and herbs. Cook this gently for 1 hour. Strain the stock, return to the pan and reduce by half. Whisk in the cream and butter. Season with salt and pepper. When ready to serve, bring back to the boil.

Prepare the puff pastry according to the instructions on page 154. Divide into 4. On a floured work surface roll out the pastry to a thickness of 3mm (⅛ in). Cut each rectangle in half. Place the mushroom parcels on 4 pieces, brush around the edges with a little egg yolk and top with the remaining pastry, pressing down carefully to seal. Refrigerate until firm.

Preheat the oven to 220°C (425°F/Gas mark 7).

Remove the pithiviers from the fridge and with a sharp knife trim around the pastry to create a nice shape. Using the tip of the knife score the top of the pithiviers for a decorative finish. Glaze with egg yolk and bake for 12 to 15 minutes. To serve, cut the pithiviers in half using a serrated knife. Place on warm plates, surround with sauce and serve.

Serves 4

PITHIVIER OF SLIPPERY JACK AND PINE MUSH-ROOMS, SAUCE MADEIRA

This is a complicated dish but the result is well worth the effort. You can layer the ingredients into single-serve moulds.

3 x 1kg (2 ¼ lb) free-range chicken barrels
2 carrots, finely chopped
1 onion, finely chopped
1 leek, finely chopped
2 sticks celery, finely chopped
1 head garlic, finely chopped
750ml (1½ pints / 3 cups) shiraz
10 large leeks
1 litre (2 pints / 4 cups) Chicken Stock (page 152)
4 beetroot, peeled and finely chopped
500g (1 lb 2 oz) foie gras
100g (3½ oz) egg whites
6 leaves gelatine

Garnish
2 beetroot
300ml (½ pint) water
200ml (7 fl oz) red wine vinegar
zest of 1 orange
2 sprigs thyme
12 coriander seeds
50ml (1¾ fl oz) olive oil

Take the chicken fillets off the bone and remove all skin and sinew. Chop the bones into small pieces. Place the fillets in a tray, and cover with carrots, onion, leek, celery, garlic and wine. Leave to marinate overnight. The next day, strain the marinade into a saucepan and bring to the boil, skimming off any scum.

Put the fillets into a pan and pour over the heated marinade. Cook in a saucepan on top of the stove at 80°C (175°F) until the chicken is just done.

Clean and blanch the 10 leeks.

Put the chicken bones in a pan and cover with stock, the red wine marinade, all the marinade vegetables and 2 of the beetroot. Cook for 1½ hours over low heat on top of the stove, then strain and cool.

Take the foie gras from the fridge 2 hours before use. It has to be soft to be moulded. Form 6 long cylinders and freeze.

Put the remaining beetroot into a food processor and blend. Add the egg whites. When the paste has come together pour into the cooled stock. Heat quickly and whisk until the stock comes to the boil and the whites form a raft. When the stock is clear, strain. Add the gelatine, season and allow to cool.

Line a 30cm x 10cm (12 in x 4 in) terrine mould with clingfilm and place in a deep baking tray. Pour ice around the mould. Pour in around 50–100ml (1¾–3½ fl oz) of jelly and allow to set. Layer the fillets, leeks and foie gras between layers of jelly until you reach the top, finishing with a layer of jelly. Refrigerate overnight.

For the garnish, boil the beetroot in their skins. When cooked, peel and dice. Bring the water, red wine vinegar, orange zest, thyme and coriander seeds to the boil. Add the diced beetroot and allow to cool. Stir in the olive oil. Season with salt and pepper.

To serve, slice a piece of terrine. Dot the diced beetroot sauce around.

Serves 4

MOSAIC OF CHICKEN, LEEK AND FOIE GRAS, RED WINE AND BEET-ROOT JELLY

This dish was inspired by Joël Robuchon's Truffle Tart, which features long caramelised onions with tiny bacon lardons on a crisp pastry disk covered in fresh Périgord truffles. If only we could afford to use truffles like this!

400g (14 oz) veal sweetbreads
olive oil and butter for pan-frying
mixed salad leaves, including mizuna, rocket,
 frisée and mâche
4 truffles, thinly sliced

Onion Compote
150g (5 oz) butter
100g (3½ oz) kaiserfleisch or bacon, julienned
6 onions, thinly sliced
50ml (1¾ fl oz) honey
50ml (1¾ fl oz) sherry vinegar

Truffle Vinaigrette
100ml (3½ fl oz) Veal Stock (page 152)
100ml (3½ fl oz) Madeira
50ml (1¾ fl oz) hazelnut oil
50ml (1¾ fl oz) truffle oil
50ml (1¾ fl oz) sherry vinegar

For the onion compote, melt the butter in a heavy-based saucepan, add the kaiserfleisch (or bacon) and onion and cook, covered, over medium heat for 5 minutes until the onions start to wilt. Remove the lid and reduce to a very low simmer for about 3 hours, stirring regularly so it doesn't catch. Remove from the heat, stir in the honey and vinegar and season to taste. Set aside.

For the truffle vinaigrette, combine the veal stock and Madeira in a saucepan and bring to the boil. Remove from the heat, whisk in the oils and vinegar, and season to taste. Set aside.

Trim the sweetbreads, removing the outer membrane. Heat a little olive oil and butter in a frying pan, add the sweetbreads and cook over high heat until crisp and golden, adding a little butter at the end. Slice the sweetbreads if large.

Toss the salad leaves with some vinaigrette.

To serve, place some compote in the centre of a serving plate. Top with the sliced truffle, then the sweetbreads and salad leaves, and drizzle the plate with a little more of the dressing.

Serves 4

ROASTED VEAL SWEET-BREADS, FRESH TRUFFLES, COMPOTE OF ONION AND HONEY, TRUFFLE VINAIG-RETTE

In England John Dory is one of the most expensive fish to buy. In Australia not only is it readily available, it is also very affordable. The flavour and texture of the roasted fish marries extremely well with the unusual sauce.

1kg (2 1/4 lb) black salsify
juice of 2 lemons
2 large John Dory
25g (1 oz) dried trompette de mort
1 head garlic, halved across
100–150ml (3 1/2–5 fl oz) olive oil
50g (1 3/4 oz) plain flour
1 sprig thyme
1 bay leaf
500g (1 lb 2 oz) spinach, picked through and washed
butter
chervil sprigs

Sauce
50g (1 3/4 oz) shallots, sliced
25ml (1 fl oz) olive oil
50g (1 3/4 oz) sliced mushrooms
140ml (5 fl oz) Sauternes
200ml (7 fl oz) Fish Stock (page 152)
100ml (3 1/2 fl oz) Veal Stock (page 152)
100ml (3 1/2 fl oz) thickened cream
100g (3 1/2 oz) high-quality unsalted butter
juice of 1 lemon

Top, tail and peel the salsify, putting the pieces in water acidulated with lemon juice as you go to stop oxidisation.

Fillet the dory, and cut each fillet into pieces. Allow 3 pieces per person. Trim them down to equal sizes (reserve the trimmings for the sauce).

Soak the dried trompette de mort in cold water for 2 to 3 hours.

For the confit garlic, preheat the oven to 80°C (175°F/Gas mark 1/4). Break the garlic into cloves (skins on). Put them in a pan and cover with cold water. Bring to the boil, then strain off the water. Repeat this process three times with fresh cold water – this will remove the bitterness in the garlic. Cover the blanched garlic with olive oil and bake in the oven for 1 hour or until totally soft.

To cook the salsify prepare a pan of salted boiling water. Make a paste with the flour and a little cold water and add to the boiling water until it has the consistency of runny thickened cream – this is a blanc that will keep the salsify white as you cook it. Cook the salsify until it is tender, about 6 minutes, and allow to cool.

For the sauce place the shallots in a pan with the olive oil. Cook over a low heat until they begin to soften, then add the mushrooms. When the mushrooms are soft, add the fish trimmings and cook without colouring for 1 to 2 minutes. Deglaze with Sauternes and reduce by two-thirds, add the fish stock and reduce by half, then add the veal stock and reduce by half. Add the cream and bring to the boil. Remove from the heat and stir in the butter with a wooden spoon until it has dissolved. Season with salt and pepper, add the lemon juice and strain through a fine sieve.

Preheat a non-stick frying pan and add some olive oil. Preheat the oven to 260°C (500°F/Gas mark 9). Season the fish and place in the pan. Add the salsify, thyme and bay leaf and place in the oven. (The cooking will usually take 3 to 4 minutes but this may vary depending on the size of the fish.)

Reheat the garlic in a little of the oil. Sauté the spinach in butter and season to taste with salt and pepper. Add some butter to another pan and sauté the drained mushrooms. Season to taste.

To serve, place a mound of sautéed spinach on a warm plate. Stack the fish and salsify on top, scatter over the mushrooms and garlic and pour the sauce over the fish. Garnish with picked chervil.

Serves 4

FINGERS OF JOHN DORY, ROASTED SALSIFY, TROMPETTE DE MORT, SAUCE, SAUTERNES

The marriage of white-fleshed birds and truffles is a classic one, it's just taken a little further here. Pour the consommé over the bird at the table so your guests can enjoy the perfume of the truffles as the vapours rise.

4 hen partridges
2 Périgord truffles, thinly sliced and juices reserved
50ml (1 3/4 fl oz) Madeira

Ravioli
250g (9 oz) assorted wild mushrooms, chopped
150g (5 oz) foie gras
2 tablespoons Chicken Mousse (page 152)
100g (3 1/2 oz) Pasta (page 154)
20 baby onions, peeled
200ml (7 fl oz) Chicken Stock (page 152)
100g (3 1/2 oz) butter
2 bunches English spinach
1 small Savoy cabbage, finely shredded
butter (extra)

Consommé
4 shallots
1kg (2 1/4 lb) assorted wild mushrooms, whole
1.5 litres (3 pints) Chicken Stock (page 152)
500ml (18 fl oz/2 cups) truffle juice
50g (1 3/4 oz) dried ceps
100ml (3 1/2 fl oz) egg whites

Clean and truss the partridges for roasting (ask your butcher to do this). Place a kitchen bag into another to create a double-layered bag. Into each bag place a bird, 1 tablespoon of the truffle juice and a large splash of Madeira. Expel all the air from the bag and tie the top tightly with string.

For the ravioli, assure that all ingredients are cold or the mixture will split. Sauté the wild mushrooms in olive oil until soft. Allow to cool. Add the foie gras to the chicken mousse and blend in a food processor until smooth. Add the mushrooms and mix well.

Roll out the pasta through the thinnest setting of your machine into a long strip, then cut in half. Place 4 truffle slices on a sheet about 10cm (4 in) apart, then top with a quarter of the mushroom filling. Cover with the second sheet of pasta, pressing down firmly to seal the edges. Cut out the ravioli using a round 6cm (2 1/2 in) pastry cutter and pinch around to ensure a good seal. Blanch the ravioli in a pan of boiling water for 30 seconds, then refresh in ice water to prevent the pasta from discolouring. Set aside.

For the consommé, sweat the shallots without colouring in some olive oil. Add the mushrooms. When wilted, add the chicken stock. Cook for 20 minutes, then strain. Add the truffle juice and allow to cool. Put the ceps in a food processor with the egg whites and blend. Stir this into the consommé and put on the heat for around 30 minutes until the whites form a raft and the stock is crystal clear.

Preheat the oven to 180°C (350°F/Gas mark 4). Peel the baby onions and cook in the oven in an emulsion of chicken stock and butter until tender, 15 to 20 minutes. Pick over and wash the spinach.

Cook the partridges in water for 20 minutes at 80°C (175°F). Allow to rest for 10 minutes, then debone the birds.

Cook the ravioli in boiling water for a further 4 minutes.

Sauté the cabbage in a little butter. In a separate pan, sauté the spinach in butter.

To serve, place a mound of cabbage on a plate and top with the partridge. Place the ravioli on a mound of spinach and scatter the onions around, then the remaining truffle slices. Pour over the boiling consommé and serve.

Serves 4

PARTRIDGE 'EN VESSIE' WITH TRUFFLE CONSOMME, WILD MUSHROOM AND FOIE GRAS RAVIOLI

This dish is a fine balance of richness and freshness, colour and texture. The carrot and chervil purée both complements and mitigates the richness of the poivrade sauce and the meat.

2 large hares

Civet
1 carrot, cut into 2cm (3/4 in) dice
1 onion, cut into 2cm (3/4 in) dice
2 sticks celery, cut into 2cm (3/4 in) dice
1 head garlic halved across,
1 bay leaf, 4–5 sprigs thyme
750ml (1 1/2 pints / 3 cups) shiraz
4 litres (8 pints) Veal Stock (page 152)

Torte
2 bunches English spinach
2 onions, diced
100g (3 1/2 oz) smoked belly bacon, diced
4 Herb Pancakes (page 152)
500g (1 lb 2 oz) Puff Pastry (page 154)
egg yolk

Sauce Poivrade
1 carrot, cut into 1cm (1/2 in) dice
1 onion, cut into 1cm (1/2 in) dice
2 sticks celery, cut into 1cm (1/2 in) dice
1 head garlic, halved across
60 crushed peppercorns
100ml (3 1/2 fl oz) raspberry vinegar
1 litre (2 pints / 4 cups) shiraz
3.5 litres (7 pints) Civet Stock
2 tablespoons redcurrant jelly
150g (5 oz) butter

Garnish
12 large carrots, peeled
1 large celeriac
butter
1 bunch chervil, chopped

Take the legs and shoulders off the hares. Remove the loins from the carcasses, discarding any sinew. Chop up the carcass and shoulder for the sauce.

For the civet, marinate the legs with carrot, onion, celery, garlic, bay leaf, thyme and shiraz for 24 hours. The next day, remove the legs from the marinade, dry with a cloth and seal in a hot pan in olive oil until golden. Strain the marinade from the vegetables and bring the liquid to the boil, skimming any scum.

Preheat the oven to 80°C (175°F/Gas mark 1/4).

Sweat the marinade vegetables in some olive oil and deglaze with the marinade. Reduce the liquid by half, add the legs and cover with veal stock. Bring to the boil, cover with a lid, and place in the oven for 6 to 8 hours. Remove from the oven and allow to cool in the liquid. When cold, take the meat off the bone and shred it with your fingers.

For the torte, wash the spinach, chop and sauté in some butter. Sweat the onion and bacon in some olive oil, then mix with the spinach and shredded meat.

Remove 100ml (3 1/2 fl oz) of the civet stock and boil hard to reduce to a glaze. Add to the spinach mixture. Place a quarter of the mixture on each pancake, wrap into a parcel and refrigerate.

Roll out the puff pastry and cut into 4. Wrap each pancake parcel in puff pastry. Refrigerate again, then using the tip of the knife score the top of the tortes for a decorative finish.

For the sauce, brown the hare bones in vegetable oil, being careful not to over-brown or the sauce will be bitter. Add the vegetables and sweat, then the peppercorns. Deglaze with the raspberry vinegar, reduce, then add the red wine and reduce by half. Pour in the civet stock and cook for 1 1/2 hours. Strain the stock and reduce by half. To finish whisk in the redcurrant jelly and butter. Season with salt and pepper.

For the garnish, slice 8 carrots into 1cm (1/2 in) rounds. Simmer in water for 1 hour until soft. Strain, put in a food processor and then push through a drum sieve. Put into a cloth and hang in the fridge for 2 to 4 hours. Cut the remaining carrots and celeriac into 2cm (3/4 in) dice.

Preheat the oven to 260°C (500°F/Gas mark 9). Seal the hare loins quickly in a very hot pan for 30 seconds on each side, then place in the oven for 1 minute. Remove and allow to rest.

Roast the diced carrot and celeriac in some butter until golden, shaking occasionally to make sure they do not catch.

Reduce the oven to 220°C (425°F/Gas mark 7). Glaze the torte with egg yolk and bake for 10 minutes. Heat the carrot purée in a pan, season and add the chervil.

To serve, place the pithivier on the plate, and spoon on some purée. Carve the hare into 12 to 14 slices and fan out on the purée. Scatter the vegetable dice around and spoon over the sauce.

Serves 4

ROAST SADDLE OF HARE, TORTE OF THE LEG, 'CIVET' WITH SAUCE POIVRADE

STEP BY STEP
FRICASSEE OF FRESHWATER MARRONS, CHESTNUT NOODLES AND TARRAGON, WHITE PORT SAUCE

The fact that the French word for confit chestnuts is the same as the name for these freshwater creatures was the initial inspiration for this dish. As it turns out the crumbly chestnut and sweet, nutty flavour of the marron is a perfect partnership.

1 large or 2 medium-sized marrons
   (allow 200−250g/7−9 oz per person)
1 clove garlic, 1 bay leaf, 1 sprig thyme,
1 leek leaf, 1 stick celery, 1 shallot
5 medium-sized carrots
150g (5 oz) butter
16 large chestnuts, peeled
20 baby onions, peeled and trimmed
250ml (9 fl oz/1 cup) Chicken Stock (page 152)
leaves from 1 bunch tarragon

Sauce
10 shallots, sliced
150g (5 oz) button mushrooms, sliced
a pinch of cayenne
375ml (13 fl oz/1¹/2 cups) white port
1 litre (2 pints/4 cups) Veal Stock (page 152)
1 litre (2 pints/4 cups) Fish Stock (page 152)
1 head garlic, halved across

Pasta
1¹/2 cups plain flour
1 cup chestnut flour
2 teaspoons gluten flour
3 eggs
1 tablespoon olive oil

PREPARE MARRONS

CUT NOODLES

Blanch the marrons in boiling salted water for 1 minute. Remove (and reserve) the heads, claws and shell. Cut the tail meat in half, discarding the vein. Refrigerate the tails until ready to use.

For the sauce, chop the heads, claws and shells and sauté in some vegetable oil over a high flame until the shells turn red and smell nutty. Sweat the shallots and mushrooms in some vegetable oil. When wilted, add the cayenne and mix in the shells. Deglaze with white port, reduce by half, then add the stocks and garlic. Cook for 1 hour. Strain and reduce by half.

For the pasta, place the flours in a food processor. Add the eggs and oil and blend until crumbly. Tip out and knead until the dough holds together. Wrap in clingfilm and allow to rest for 2 hours at room temperature.

Make a bouquet garni by wrapping the garlic, bay leaf and thyme in a leek leaf and tie with string. Chop the celery, half a carrot and shallot into small dice and sweat in 50g (1¾ oz) butter. Add the bouquet garni, chestnuts and onions, and after 10 minutes the rest of the sliced carrots. Cover with stock and simmer until tender. Remove the chestnuts.

Roll out the pasta through the thinnest setting on your machine, then cut into tagliatelle.

In a pan, put 50g (1¾ oz) butter, the tarragon and marrons. Heat gently until the marrons are just cooked.

Cook the pasta in lots of boiling water until it rises to the surface. Season and roll through some melted butter and twirl into balls.

To serve, place a ball of pasta at the top of the plate. Arrange the marron below then scatter the onions, carrots and chestnuts over and around. Bring the sauce to the boil and whisk in 50g (1¾ oz) butter. Pour evenly over the marrons and serve immediately.

Serves 4

COOK
GARNISH

SAUTE
MARRONS

'Season of mists and mellow fruitfulness' . . . a culinary equivalent of Keats' 'Ode to Autumn'.

Confit Zest (page 156)

Quince
1 quantity Quince Syrup (page 108)
8 quinces, peeled, quartered, cored

Pear
400g (14 oz) caster sugar
1 litre (2 pints) water
6 pears, peeled, halved, cored

Apricot
12 dried apricots
300g (10 3/4 oz) caster sugar
1 litre (2 pints/4 cups) water

Prunes
200g (7 oz) unpitted prunes
100g (3 1/2 oz) sultanas
600g (1 lb 5 oz) caster sugar
1 litre (2 pints/4 cups) water
40ml (1 1/2 fl oz) Armagnac

Vanilla Ice-cream
1 vanilla bean
200ml (7 fl oz) milk
300ml (1/2 pint) cream
105g (4 oz) caster sugar
6 egg yolks
100ml (3 1/2 fl oz) cream (extra)

Muscat Ice-cream
110g (4 oz) egg yolks
125ml (4 fl oz/1/2 cup) Sugar Syrup
 (page 156)
1 teaspoon grated orange zest
180ml (6 1/2 fl oz) liqueur muscat
250ml (9 fl oz/1 cup) cream

Quince Sorbet
4 of the poached quinces
150ml (5 fl oz) water

Prepare the quince syrup according to the instructions on page 108. Drop in the quinces and reduce the heat to barely a simmer. Poach on very low heat for about 4 hours or until the quinces are a deep red. Allow to cool in the syrup. Reserve 200ml (7 fl oz) of the syrup for the quince sorbet.

To poach the pears, bring the sugar and water to the boil. Place the pears in the syrup, press a circle of baking paper on top and weigh down with a plate. Reduce the heat to barely a simmer and poach until tender. Allow to cool in the syrup.

Soak the apricots in boiling water for 1 hour. Make a syrup with the sugar and water, bring to the boil and add the soaked apricots. Reduce the heat and poach for 15 minutes.

Pour enough boiling water over the prunes to cover. Soak for 1 hour. Add the sultanas. Make a syrup with the sugar and water. Bring to the boil and add the soaked fruit. Reduce the heat and poach for 15 minutes. Remove from the heat and pour off half the syrup. Top up with Armagnac and refrigerate until needed.

For the vanilla ice-cream, scrape the seeds from the vanilla bean and put both in a pan with the milk and cream. Bring to the boil. Whisk the sugar into the yolks until pale and thick, then pour the milk and cream onto the yolks, whisking continuously. Return to the pan and gently heat until it reaches 80°C (175°F) or is thick enough to coat the spoon. Do not boil. Cool the custard completely in a metal bowl with the vanilla bean. When cold, strain, then add the extra cream. Refrigerate overnight and churn in an ice-cream machine according to the manufacturer's instructions 1 hour before serving.

For the muscat ice-cream, put the yolks in the bowl of an electric mixer. In a small saucepan heat the sugar syrup to 110°C (230°F) then start beating the yolks. When the syrup gets to 118°C (245°F) pour in a thin stream down the side of the bowl into the yolks. Whisk until cold, then add the orange zest and muscat. Whisk in the cream and churn in an ice-cream machine according to the manufacturer's instructions.

For the quince sorbet, purée the quince and poaching syrup and pass through a fine sieve. Add the water and churn in an ice-cream machine according to the manufacturer's instructions.

To serve spoon some poached fruit onto a plate and place a scoop of each ice-cream at the bottom. Spoon some syrup over the fruit and serve.

Serves 6

COMPOTE OF AUTUMN FRUITS WITH QUINCE SORBET, MUSCAT, AND VANILLA ICE-CREAMS

Passionfruit are at their best in autumn. The combination of this divine, slightly acidic chocolate and passionfruit is a surprising triumph. It's a visual treat as well.

Tempered Chocolate (page 154)
1/2 quantity Chocolate Sponge (page 154)
1/4 quantity Passionfruit Sorbet (page 156)

Chocolate Sabayon
210g (7 1/2 oz) Manjari or best-quality chocolate
2 egg yolks
1 egg
90g (3 oz) caster sugar
300ml (10 1/2 fl oz) lightly whipped cream

Pears
6 ripe but firm pears (Packham or Bartlett)
1 quantity Sugar Syrup (page 156)
pulp from 24 passionfruit

You will need 6 to 8 pyramid moulds or dessert rings of 150ml (5 fl oz) capacity for this recipe.

For the sabayon chop the chocolate finely with a serrated knife. Place in a metal bowl and set over a pan of barely simmering water, stirring often until melted. Keep warm.

Put the egg yolks and egg in the bowl of an electric mixer. In a small saucepan, dissolve the sugar in 1 tablespoon water, then brush the sides of the saucepan with a damp pastry brush. Bring to 112°C (225°F) (use a sugar thermometer) then start beating in the eggs in the mixer. When the syrup reaches 118°C (250°F) remove from the heat, allow the bubbles to die down slightly, then pour in a thin stream down the side of the bowl into the eggs. Continue whisking until cold.

Fold a third of the whipped cream into the warm chocolate (the chocolate must be quite warm, about 50°C (122°F), or it will set too quickly), then fold in the egg mixture and the rest of the cream.

Immediately divide the mixture into the pyramids or dessert moulds and smooth the surfaces with a palette knife. Refrigerate for at least 2 hours.

For the pears, using a parisienne scoop or melon baller, remove the core and a little flesh from the base, taking care not to get too close to the skin. Peel the pears and trim the stalks to an attractive length. Bring the sugar syrup to the boil and add the pears. Press a circle of baking paper down on the surface of the syrup. Reduce the heat to a simmer and continue poaching until the pears are tender. Allow to cool in the syrup.

Whiz the passionfruit pulp briefly in a food processor, then pass through a fine sieve. Drain off half the pear poaching syrup and top up with passionfruit juice. Refrigerate for at least 4 hours.

Temper the chocolate according to the instructions on page 154. Wet a work surface slightly and smooth a piece of chocolate paper or acetate on it. Using a long palette knife spread a thin even layer of melted chocolate over the paper. Just before it sets hard, cut—using a stencil of the pyramid side and a dull-edged knife—into triangles. There is no need to cut through the paper, so be gentle. Flip the whole sheet over onto a tray to prevent the edges curling up as the chocolate contracts.

Using the same stencil, cut out 6 to 8 pieces of sponge to fit the pyramid bases. Press on to the sabayon. Dip the moulds into hot water and gently ease out the mousse by inserting a thin-bladed knife along one side of the mould. Slide the pyramid out and place on a plate. Gently peel the chocolate triangles off the paper and place against the pyramid. Using a piping bag, pipe some passionfruit sorbet into the cavity of each pear. Place next to a pyramid and pour a little of the pear syrup around. Serve immediately.

Serves 6–8

PYRAMID OF VALRHONA'S MANJARI CHOCOLATE WITH A PEAR POACHED IN PASSIONFRUIT JUICE

Perfectly ripe fruit in season need little embellishment.
Hot sweet fruit, crisp buttery pastry and boozy cream;
the perfect finisher on a cool autumn's night.

400g (14 oz) caster sugar
750ml (1 1/2 pints/3 cups) water
250ml (9 fl oz/1 cup) muscat
1 vanilla bean
12 ripe figs
1/4 quantity Puff Pastry (page 154)
120ml (4 1/4 fl oz) muscat, reduced by half (extra)
200ml (7 fl oz) whipped cream
icing sugar

Bring to the boil the sugar, water, muscat and vanilla.
Add the figs and reduce the heat. Poach for 8 to 10
minutes, then remove from the syrup. Continue boiling
the syrup until reduced by half. Reserve and warm
before use.

Prepare the pastry following the instructions on page
154 and roll out to a thickness of about 4mm (1/8 in).
Cut into circles just slightly larger than the circumference
of the figs. Refrigerate for 30 minutes.

Fold the reduced muscat into the whipped cream.

Preheat the oven to 190°C (375°F/Gas mark 5).

Put the pastry disks on a lined baking tray and with a
fork prick all over the base. Using a sharp knife, slice a
little off the stalk end of the figs. Put them cut-side down
on the pastry, dust heavily with icing sugar and bake
until the pastry is golden, 10 to 12 minutes.

To serve, put 2 tarts on each plate and spoon over some
of the fig syrup. Serve the cream on the side if you wish.

Serves 6

HOT FIG TARTS WITH MUSCAT CREAM

A long-standing favourite and the best-selling dessert at est est est. Ice-cream tastes better if it is made the day before.

Truffle Centre
170g (6 oz) Pur Caraibe or
  best-quality bitter chocolate
115ml (4 fl oz) cream

Almond Ice-cream
1 litre (2 pints/4 cups) milk
200g (7 oz) toasted flaked almonds
200ml (7 fl oz) cream
180g (6 1/2 oz) caster sugar
12 egg yolks
200ml (7 fl oz) cream (extra)
50ml (1 3/4 fl oz) Amaretto

Caramel Sauce
150g (5 oz) caster sugar
80ml (2 3/4 oz) water
20ml (3/4 oz) Amaretto

Praline
100g (3 1/2 oz) toasted flaked almonds
100g (3 1/2 oz) caster sugar

Soufflé
225g (8 oz) chocolate
50g (1 3/4 oz) softened butter
200g (7 oz) egg whites
65g (2 oz) caster sugar
50g (1 3/4 oz) egg yolks

You will need 8 metal dessert rings that measure 7cm x 3.5cm (2 3/4 in x 1 3/4 in).

For the truffle centre, grate the chocolate finely with the heel of a large knife and place in a metal bowl. Bring the cream to the boil and pour over the chocolate. Stir until smooth and shiny. Pour into a small tray lined with baking paper and freeze. Cut into 4cm (1 1/2 in) squares.

For the almond ice-cream, bring the milk to the boil and add the almonds. Allow to infuse for 15 minutes. In a blender whiz the milk and almonds until puréed. Line a conical strainer with 2 layers of muslin and pour in the almond milk. Allow to drip through until the almond appears pasty. Bring the corners of the muslin together and squeeze the remaining milk out of the paste.

Measure the milk — you should have about 800ml (1 3/4 pints). Add enough cream to make up 1 litre (2 pints/4 cups) liquid. Return to the heat. In a bowl sprinkle the sugar onto the egg yolks, whisking as you go until the mixture is thick and pale yellow. Dribble in the hot almond milk while still whisking. Return the mixture to the saucepan and cook over medium heat until it reaches 80°C (175°F) or coats the back of a spoon. Strain into a large bowl and allow to cool completely, stirring occasionally. When cold add the extra cream and Amaretto. Refrigerate. Churn 1 hour before needed.

For the soufflés, line a baking tray with baking paper. Cut extra baking paper into 18cm x 6cm (7 in x 2 1/2 in) strips. Spray the dessert rings with canola oil, line with the strips and spray again.

Finely chop the chocolate and set over a pan of barely simmering water. Stir until melted then add the butter. Turn off the heat but leave the bowl in place to keep warm. Start beating the egg whites. When they are white and just holding their shape, sprinkle in the sugar and continue beating until firm, taking care not to over-beat. Remove the chocolate from the heat and quickly stir in the egg yolks, then a third of the whites. Fold in the remaining whites, taking care not to overmix. Put the mixture into a piping bag and carefully pipe approximately 1 tablespoon-sized blobs into the rings. Drop a truffle square onto the soufflé, then pipe around and on top of it until you reach the top of the rings (not the paper). Refrigerate for 1 hour.

For the praline, put a heavy-bottomed saucepan on moderate heat. When quite hot sprinkle in a little of the sugar. Once this has dissolved, stir in a little more sugar. Continue until all the sugar is used up and you have a light caramel. Add the nuts and stir to coat them, then tip onto baking paper and allow to cool and harden. Pulverise roughly in a food processor.

Preheat the oven to 180°C (350°F/Gas mark 4). For the sauce, caramelise the sugar and 30ml (1 fl oz) water in a saucepan. Remove from the heat and pour in the remaining water bit by bit. (Take care as it will splutter.) Once the water is incorporated add the Amaretto. Return to the heat and let it bubble for a minute, then allow to cool.

Place the soufflés in the oven and cook for 12 minutes. While the soufflés are cooking, dribble a ring of sauce around the plates and put a little pile of praline where you will be placing the ice-cream. Remove the soufflés from the rings by putting a wide palette knife under each and gently lifting off the ring, leaving the paper collar in place. Transfer the soufflé to the plate, then peel off the paper. Dip a spoon in warm water and spoon an egg-shaped scoop of ice-cream on the plate and serve.

Serves 4

SOUFFLE OF VALR- HONA'S PUR CARAIBE CHOCO- LATE, ALMOND ICE- CREAM, SAUCE CARA- MEL

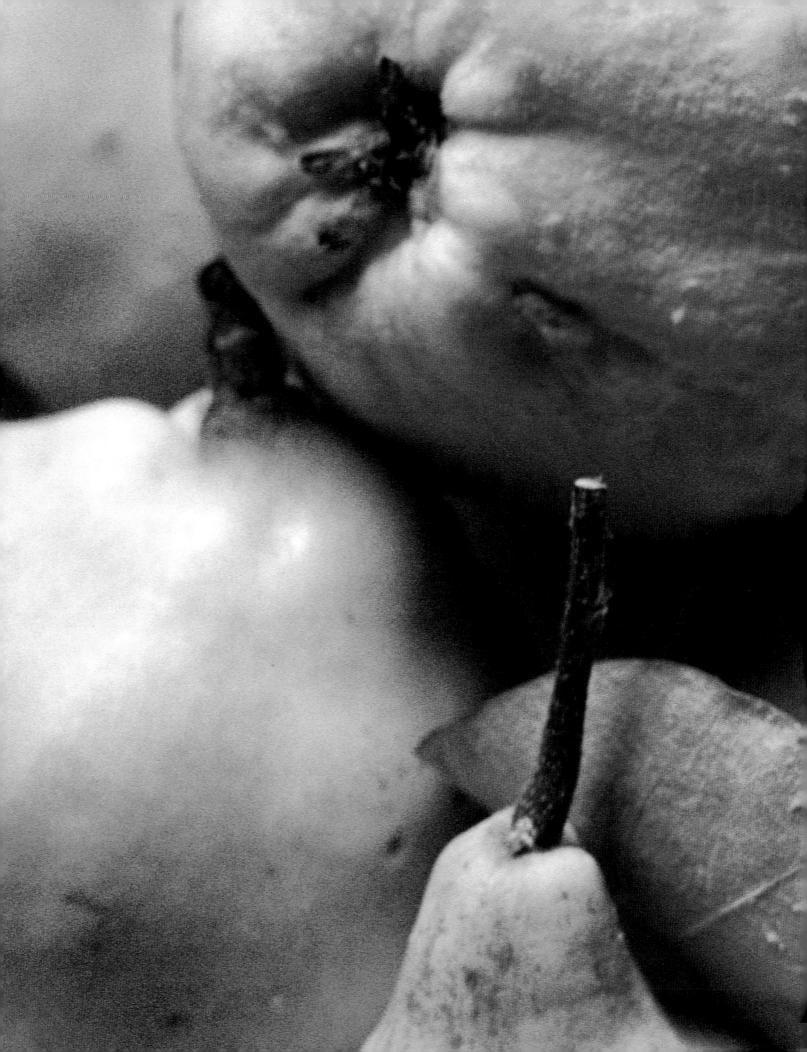

On a dreary winter's evening this light, colourful dish will lift the spirits of your guests and remind them that spring is on its way.

2 rainbow trout
rock salt
250g (9 oz) pink fir apple potatoes
1 bulb baby fennel, finely sliced
plain flour
vegetable oil for frying
300ml (1/2 pint) Fish Stock (page 152)
100ml (3 1/2 fl oz) Mayonnaise (page 152)
juice of 1/2 lemon
100ml (3 1/2 fl oz) lightly whipped cream
2 ripe avocados
Osietra caviar
chive batons

Fillet the rainbow trout and cover the fillets with rock salt. Allow to sit for 5 to 10 minutes, then rinse under cold water. Smoke the fillets, skin-side down, in a small fish smoker filled with hickory for 2 to 3 minutes. Cool.

Boil the potatoes in their skins. Cool and slice into 5mm (1/4 in) rounds.

Lightly flour the fennel and fry in hot oil until crisp.

Reduce the fish stock to a glaze, add the mayonnaise and lemon juice. Season with salt and pepper, then fold in the cream. Adjust the seasoning.

Remove the skin from the fish and break each fillet into 3 pieces.

Halve the avocado, remove the stone, peel and cut into 5mm (1/4 in) slices. Put 2 slices of potato on the serving plate, followed by a slice of avocado, a little deep-fried fennel and the fish. Repeat the layers with the rest of the ingredients.

Spoon over the dressing and place some caviar on top. Garnish with the fennel and chive batons.

Serves 4

SALAD OF SMOKED RAINBOW TROUT WITH PINK FIR APPLE POTATOES, AVOCADO AND OSIETRA CAVIAR

Counteract the incredible sweetness of blue swimmer crab with the savoury flavour of celery and the earthy fragrance of black truffles.

4 blue swimmer crabs
6 scallops
1 egg white
150ml (5 fl oz) cream
cayenne
juice of 1 lemon
150g (5 oz) Pasta (page 154)

Sauce
1 head celeriac
1 head celery, leaves reserved
100g (3½ oz) butter
1.5 litres (3 pints) Vegetable Nage (page 152)
200ml (7 fl oz) cream
celery salt
50ml (1¾ fl oz) Chicken Stock (page 152)
50g (1¾ oz) butter
4 teaspoons chopped truffle
2 teaspoons truffle oil

Tempura Batter
1 tablespoon rice flour
1 tablespoon plain flour
2 egg whites, whipped
a drop of white wine vinegar

Remove the meat from the raw crabs, making sure to remove all shell and cartilage. Chop slightly. Refrigerate.

Make a mousse by blending the scallops in a food processor until smooth. With the machine still running add the egg white and the cream. Transfer to a bowl and fold in the crab meat. Season with salt and cayenne and add the lemon juice. Refrigerate.

Prepare the pasta according to the instructions on page 154 and roll out as thinly as possible. Cut out 20 x 6cm (2½ in) rounds. Place 1 teaspoon filling on the bottom half of the pasta round, and fold down the top to make a semi-circle. Press to seal the edge, then twist the 2 ends together to form a tortellini. Repeat with the rest of the pasta and filling.

For the sauce, chop two-thirds of the celeriac and celery into small pieces and sweat in butter until soft. Deglaze with the nage, then reduce by two-thirds. Strain. Add the cream and bring to the boil. Season with salt, pepper and celery salt. Set aside and reheat gently before serving.

Julienne the remaining celery and celeriac and cook in an emulsion of chicken stock and butter on top of the stove without colouring. When al dente add the truffle and truffle oil and season.

Make the tempura batter by combining all of the ingredients. Rest for 30 minutes before use. Dip the celery leaves into the batter and deep-fry in vegetable oil until crisp. Drain well and season with salt.

To serve place 5 tortellini on each plate with a generous portion of julienne vegetables. Garnish with 3 celery leaves, pour over the sauce and serve. Top with a sliced truffle if you like.

Serves 4

TORTELLINI OF BLUE SWIMMER CRAB, WINTER TRUFFLES, CELERY NAGE

This is our up-market version of the old favourite, bangers and beans.

4 shallots, finely diced
2 cloves garlic, finely diced
250g (9 oz) button mushrooms, whole
1 handful trompette de mort, soaked
250g (9 oz) foie gras, finely diced
1 quantity Chicken Mousse (page 152)
four spices (quartre-épices)
sausage skin
2 bunches Dutch carrots, peeled
100ml (3½ fl oz) duck fat
½ onion, sliced

Duck Confit
4 duck legs
100g (3½ oz) rock salt
4 sprigs thyme, chopped
1 bay leaf, chopped
2 litres (4 pints) duck fat

Cassoulet
500g (1 lb 2 oz) white beans,
  soaked overnight
2–3 litres (4–6 pints) Chicken Stock
  (page 152)
2 onions, left whole
2 carrots, left whole
2 sticks celery, left whole
2 leeks, left whole
2 heads garlic, left whole
1 sprig thyme, 1 bay leaf

Sauce
500g (1 lb 2 oz) duck bones, chopped
10 shallots, finely sliced
1 head garlic, halved across
250g (9 oz) button mushrooms, sliced
2 tablespoons red wine vinegar
375ml (13 fl oz/1½ cups) ruby port
500ml (18 fl oz/2 cups) Veal Stock
  (page 152)
500ml (18 fl oz/2 cups) Chicken Stock
  (page 152)
2 sprigs thyme, 1 bay leaf
100g (3½ oz) butter

Salad
1 teaspoon Dijon mustard
100ml (3½ fl oz) walnut oil
50ml (1¾ fl oz) sherry vinegar
3 apples, peeled and cut
  into batons

BOUDIN OF DUCK CONFIT AND FOIE GRAS, CASSOULET OF WHITE BEANS, APPLE SALAD, PORT SAUCE

For the confit, salt the duck legs overnight with the rock salt, thyme and bay leaf. The next day, wash the salt off the legs.

Preheat the oven to 80°C (175°F/Gas mark ¼). Melt the duck fat, submerge the legs in the fat and cook for 4 to 6 hours. When cooked (the meat should fall off the bone) allow to cool in the fat. Remove the meat from the bone and chop slightly.

Sweat the shallots and garlic in some butter, then add the button mushrooms. Cook until all the moisture has evaporated. Blend the mushroom mixture in a food processor with the trompette de mort until you have a fine paste.

Freeze the foie gras. Gently fold the mushrooms, chicken mousse, duck meat and foie gras together. Season with salt, pepper and four spices. Allow to set slightly in the fridge. Fry some of the mixture to test for seasoning and adjust accordingly.

For the cassoulet, cook the beans in the stock with the vegetables, thyme and bay leaf for 2 to 2½ hours or until tender. Remove the vegetables and leave the beans to cool in the stock.

Preheat the oven to 260°C (500°F/Gas mark 9).

For the sauce, roast the duck bones until golden. Sweat the shallots, garlic and mushrooms in vegetable oil until golden brown. Deglaze with the vinegar, then add two-thirds of the port. Reduce to a glaze. Add the stocks and bring to the boil. Add the bones, thyme and bay leaf and simmer for 1 hour. Strain. Reduce the remaining port by half and add to the sauce. Bring to the boil, then add the butter. Set aside and bring to the boil before serving.

Take the mousse from the fridge and put it into a piping bag or sausage machine. Roll the sausage skin onto the nozzle, making sure there are no air bubbles. Tie the sausages into 5cm (2 in) lengths, poach for 4 to 5 minutes in simmering water, then cool. Remove the skin from the sausages, slice diagonally into 5 and chargrill.

Sweat the carrots in the duck fat, then add the onion, some of the bean stock and the beans. Season with salt and pepper.

For the salad combine the mustard, oil and vinegar and toss in the apples to coat.

To serve, place the beans in a bowl and top with the sliced sausage. Place the apple in the middle. Spoon the sauce around.

Serves 6

If you wish to serve this sumptuous dish as the starter of three courses, keep the other dishes relatively light.

12 thin slices pancetta

Ravioli
4 jumbo quail
10g (1/2 oz) Chicken Mousse (page 152)
80g (2 3/4 oz) foie gras
8 large spinach leaves
150g (5 oz) Pasta (page 154)

Brussels Sprout Purée
20 Brussels sprouts
10g (1/2 oz) butter
50ml (1 3/4 fl oz) cream

Sauce
4 shallots, finely chopped
1 carrot, finely chopped
1/2 leek, finely chopped
1 stick celery, finely chopped
1 sprig thyme
1 bay leaf
1 head garlic, halved across
250ml (9 fl oz/1 cup) white wine
150ml (5 fl oz) Chicken Stock (page 152)
150ml (5 fl oz) Veal Stock (page 152)

For the ravioli, take the quail breasts off the bone and remove the skin. (Reserve the bones and carcasses for the sauce.) Using a meat bat, slightly flatten the breasts. Season and smear with the chicken mousse. Cut the foie gras into 4 equal pieces and place on top of 4 breast pieces. Cover with the other 4 quail breasts.

Blanch the spinach leaves and refresh.

Prepare the pasta according to instructions on page 152 and roll out through the thinnest setting of your machine. Wrap each quail parcel in spinach, then in pasta. Blanch the parcels for 30 seconds in boiling water and refresh.

For the Brussels sprout purée, first remove 24 of the greenest sprout leaves for garnish. Slice the remaining sprouts really finely then sweat quickly in butter. When softened add the cream, bring to the boil and liquidise until smooth. Chill.

Preheat the oven to 260°C (500°F/Gas mark 9).

For the sauce chop the quail carcasses and roast in the oven for 15 minutes until golden brown. Sweat the shallots, carrot, leek and celery in some vegetable oil, add the herbs and garlic, then deglaze with the white wine. When reduced to a glaze, add the stocks. Simmer for 1 hour. Strain. The sauce should be reduced by a third, and be more like a jus than a sauce.

Cook the pancetta in a little olive oil until crispy. Cook the ravioli in boiling salted water for 3 minutes. Rest for 2 minutes. Reheat the purée in a saucepan. Quickly blanch the remaining Brussels sprout leaves.

To serve, place a mound of purée on the plate and the ravioli on top. Garnish with the Brussels sprout leaves and crispy pancetta. Spoon the sauce around.

Serves 4

RAVIOLI OF QUAIL AND FOIE GRAS, BRUSSELS SPROUT PUREE, WHITE WINE JUS

Fish cooked in this way stays moist and succulent. The unusual combination of flavours will both surprise and delight.

800g (1¾ lb) tuna loin, trimmed of sinew
4 baby cabbages, leaves separated
1 bunch garlic chives, trimmed but left whole

Stock
1 smoked ham hock
1 head fennel, coarsely chopped
2 carrots, coarsely chopped
2 sticks celery, coarsely chopped
½ onion, coarsely chopped
2 litres (4 pints) Chicken Stock (page 152)
4 star anise
1 bay leaf
4 sprigs thyme
1 tablespoon fennel seeds

Pomme Boulangère
3 shallots, finely diced
2 cloves garlic, finely diced
50ml (1¾ fl oz) olive oil
3 potatoes, cut into cylinders and thinly sliced
100ml (3½ fl oz) Fish Stock (page 152)

Confit Shallots
20 shallots
50g (1¾ oz) butter
150ml (5 fl oz) Fish Stock (page 152)

Horseradish Cream
1 small stick horseradish, finely grated
100ml (3½ fl oz) whipped cream
lemon juice

For the stock, place the ham hock in a pot with the vegetables and cover with stock. Bring to the boil. Add the star anise, bay leaf, thyme and fennel seeds and cook slowly for 2 hours. The stock should be an amber colour. Strain and set aside.

Trim the tuna into 180 to 200g (6½ to 7 oz) steaks and set aside.

Preheat the oven to 180°C (350°F/Gas mark 4).

For the Pomme Boulangère, sweat the shallots and garlic in olive oil but do not colour. In a lined medium-sized baking tray arrange the potato slices into small concentric circles with the sides over-lapping like the petals of a flower. Place a slice of potato in the middle of each circle and a teaspoonful of the shallot mixture on top. Repeat with another over-lapping layer of potato. Make 4 in this way. Cover with fish stock and cook in the oven for 5 to 8 minutes. Keep warm.

For the confit shallots, cook the shallots in the oven at 180°C in a butter and fish stock emulsion. Blanch the cabbage leaves in boiling salted water. Reheat the ham hock stock.

For the horseradish cream, fold the horseradish into the cream. Season with salt and pepper and finish with lemon juice. Whisk until smooth.

Pan-fry the tuna for around 30 seconds on one side. Place the browned side into the ham hock bouillon to finish cooking, 1 to 2 minutes. The tuna should remain rare.

Place the potato in the serving bowl. Scatter with the cabbage leaves and shallots. Just before the tuna is ready add the garlic chives to the bouillon. Remove tuna from bouillon and place in the bowl. Pour over some hot bouillon and grind some pepper and salt over the top. Serve with horseradish cream on the side.

Serves 4

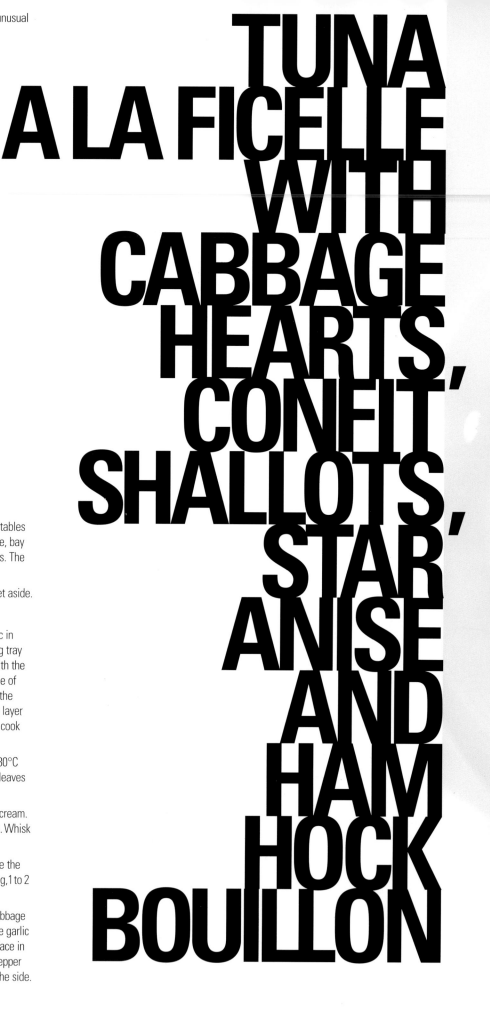

TUNA A LA FICELLE WITH CABBAGE HEARTS, CONFIT SHALLOTS, STAR ANISE AND HAM HOCK BOUILLON

ROASTED PIGEON, BABY ARTICHOKES, SAUTÉED SPINACH, SAUCE, CHUTNEY

A perfectly roasted pigeon is always a pleasure, but the sauce is the highlight of this dish. The melding of sweet, spicy and tangy is also lovely with other dark-fleshed birds such as wild duck. The quantities for the chutney will leave you with some left over, but it keeps for a long time if refrigerated.

4 plump pigeons
4 bunches spinach, picked and washed
butter

Chutney
100g (3½ oz) lemons, seeds removed and very thinly sliced
Sugar Syrup (page 156) to cover
1 tablespoon water
50g (1¾ oz) julienned ginger
375g (13 oz) Granny Smith apples,
  cored, cut into eighths and thinly sliced
50g (1¾ oz) currants
1 teaspoon salt
30g (1 oz) mustard seeds
2 dried chillies, chopped
1 clove garlic, chopped
125g (4½ oz) brown sugar
250ml (9 fl oz/1 cup) white wine vinegar

Sauce
pigeon bones
1 carrot, chopped
1 leek, chopped
1 stick celery, chopped
1 onion, chopped
1 clove garlic, halved across
100ml (3½ fl oz) white wine
200ml (7 fl oz) Veal Stock (page 152)
100ml (3½ fl oz) Chicken Stock
  (page 152)
2 sprigs thyme, 1 bay leaf
20ml (¾ fl oz) cream
10g (½ oz) butter

Artichokes
16 small globe artichokes
4 shallots, sliced
2 cloves garlic, sliced
100ml (3½ fl oz) olive oil
50ml (1¾ fl oz) white wine
10 coriander seeds, whole
1 sprig thyme, 1 bay leaf
100ml (3½ fl oz) Chicken Stock
  (page 152)
10 ground pink peppercorns

Rösti
4 Bintje potatoes
2 tablespoons clarified butter

Get your butcher to draw and truss the pigeons for roasting. Reserve the neck and winglets for the sauce.

For the chutney, blanch the lemons in boiling water 3 times (change the water after each time), then cook in the sugar syrup and water until confit, 20 to 25 minutes. Repeat with the ginger. Put the rest of the ingredients into a pan and bring to the boil. Allow to cool and sit for 1 day.

For the sauce, brown the pigeon bones in vegetable oil, then add the vegetables and garlic and sweat. Deglaze with white wine. Cover with the stocks, add the herbs and cook for 30 minutes then strain. Bring to the boil, then weigh the stock. Add an equal amount of the chutney to the stock, stir, then stir in the cream and butter.

Turn the artichokes with a knife, removing all the outside leaves, but keeping the stalks intact. Cook the shallots and garlic in olive oil without colouring until soft then add the artichokes, white wine, coriander seeds, thyme and bay leaf. Cover with the chicken stock and cook for 6 to 8 minutes or until tender. Remove the chokes with a spoon.

For the rösti, cut the potatoes into cylinders. Cut into 3mm (⅛ in) slices. Arrange 2 layers in small non-stick frying pans. Add the clarified butter to each pan, place on the heat and cook until the potatoes are golden brown on both sides.

Preheat the oven to 260°C (500°F/Gas mark 9). Roast the pigeon in the oven for about 8 minutes. Allow to rest for 10 minutes. Remove the meat from the bone. Reheat the artichokes in their cooking liquor. When hot, drain and dust with ground peppercorns. Sauté the spinach in butter.

To serve, put the potatoes in the centre of the plate, then the spinach. Cross the pigeon legs and arrange the artichokes on the side. Top with the breast meat and nap generously with the sauce.

Serves 4

Has corned beef ever looked so good? It's wonderful for a one-dish dinner party, just follow with a light dessert or cheese.

1 corned silverside
Chicken Stock (page 152) to cover
4 carrots, whole
2 onions, whole
1/2 head celery, whole
2 leeks, whole
4 heads garlic, halved across
1 bunch thyme
2 bay leaves
150ml (5 fl oz) cream
2 tablespoons grain mustard

Dumplings
2 potatoes
50g (1 3/4 oz) plain flour
1 egg
a pinch of nutmeg

Beignets
2 bone marrow shafts
2 tablespoons plain flour
2 tablespoons cornflour
1 teaspoon white wine vinegar
2 egg whites, whisked to soft peaks

Garnish
12 young Dutch carrots, peeled
4 young leeks, as thick as a thumb
12 baby turnips, peeled
1 head celeriac, peeled and cut into 2cm (3/4 in) barrels
1 baby cabbage, leaves separated

POT AU FEU OF BEEF AND ROOT VEGETABLES, BONE MARROW BEIGNETS AND A GRAIN MUSTARD SAUCE

Tie the beef silverside in the middle with string. Place in a pot of cold water and bring to the boil. Drain and rinse the meat. Place in a casserole and cover with chicken stock. Bring to the boil. Place all the vegetables and herbs in the pan with the beef and poach slowly at 80°C (175°F) for 8 hours. Allow to cool in the liquid.

Preheat the oven to 260°C (500°F/Gas mark 9).

For the dumplings, bake the unpeeled potatoes in the oven until well done. Scrape out all the flesh and pass through a drum sieve. Work the flour into the potato, then add the egg. Season with salt, pepper and nutmeg. Shape into thumb-sized dumplings. Blanch in boiling water until they float to the top, then refresh in ice water.

For the beignets, take the marrow out of the shaft and soak in cold water overnight. Cut into 2cm (3/4 in) lengths.

Combine the two flours and mix in the vinegar. Fold the egg whites into the flour mixture. Season. Set aside.

Cook all the garnish vegetables in the stock from poaching the beef until tender. Take the beef from the cooking liquid, remove the string and cut into portions. Strain the stock. Place the beef in a saucepan with the garnish vegetables and dumplings and cover with the cooking liquid. Reheat without boiling. When the meat and vege-tables are hot, remove from the pot. Reduce the stock by half and stir in the cream and mustard. Do not bring back to the boil.

Season the bone marrow. Dip into the batter and deep-fry for 1 to 2 minutes. Drain well.

To serve, place a portion of beef in the middle of the serving bowl. Surround with the vegetables and dumplings and pour the stock around. Garnish with the marrow beignet.

Serves 4

You can make this dish vegetarian by substituting some beaten egg for the chicken mousse and using vegetable stock in place of the chicken.

1 carrot, cut into brunoise
1 stick celery, cut into brunoise
1 leek, cut into brunoise
50g (1¾ oz) butter
500g (1lb 2 oz) English spinach
4 teaspoons truffle oil

Tortellini
100g (3½ oz) morels
100g (3½ oz) pine mushrooms
100g (3½ oz) dried ceps
100g (3½ oz) slippery jacks
100g (3½ oz) Swiss browns
3 shallots, chopped
2 cloves garlic, chopped
100g (3½ oz) Chicken Mousse (page 152)
1 bunch chives, chopped
250g (9 oz) Pasta (page 154)

Lentils
500g (1lb 2 oz) du Puy lentils
2 litres (4 pints) Chicken Stock (page 152)
1 onion, whole
1 carrot, whole
1 stick celery, whole
1 leek, whole
1 head garlic, halved across
1 sprig thyme
1 bay leaf
100ml (3½ fl oz) cream
50g (1¾ oz) butter

For the tortellini, reserve a few of each type of mushroom for garnishing and chop the rest. Sauté the mushrooms with the shallots and garlic in olive oil. Tip out of the pan, drain and allow to cool completely. Chop roughly and mix with the chicken mousse and chives. Refrigerate.

Prepare the pasta following the instructions on page 154 and roll out as thinly as possible. Cut into 6cm (2½ in) rounds. Place 1 teaspoon filling on the bottom half of the pasta round, and fold down the top to make a semi-circle. Press to seal the edge, then twist the 2 ends together to form a tortellini. Repeat with the rest of the pasta and filling.

Place the lentils in a pan and cover with the chicken stock. Add the rest of the ingredients except the cream and butter and cook for 25 to 30 minutes or until the lentils are just tender. Take out about a third of the lentils and reserve. Cook the rest for another 10 minutes, then remove the vegetables and blend the lentils in a food processor until smooth. Pass through a drum sieve, add the cream and butter, season and pass through a fine sieve. (Thin with a little chicken stock if the mixture is too thick.)

Sweat the brunoise vegetables in a little butter without colouring. Add the reserved whole lentils and season.

Cook the tortellini in boiling salted water for 3 to 4 minutes.

Sauté the spinach in butter. Sauté the reserved mushrooms.

To serve, scatter the lentils and vegetables in the bottom of the serving dish. Place 5 mounds of spinach on the plate, then the tortellini on top. Reheat the sauce, and just before pouring, whisk briskly so that it's foamy. Drizzle with truffle oil. Top with mushrooms.

Serves 4

TORTELLINI OF WILD MUSHROOMS, VELOUTÉ OF DU PUY LENTILS, WHITE TRUFFLE OIL

When you pour the hot syrup over the tart and present it to your guests listen to them sigh as they breathe in the spicy candy aromas rising from their plates. You can purchase the honey cake from good delicatessens.

1 ripe pineapple
½ quantity Puff Pastry (page 154)
icing sugar

Gingerbread Ice-cream

250g (9 oz) honey cake
1 litre (2 pints/4 cups) milk
2 cinnamon sticks
2 pinches four spices (quartre-épices)
2 vanilla beans, split and scraped
150ml (5 fl oz) honey
25g (¾ oz) caster sugar
12 egg yolks
300ml (10½ fl oz) cream

Spice Syrup

60g (2 oz) butter
2 tablespoons chopped fresh ginger
1 cinnamon stick
1 vanilla bean
100g (3½ oz) caster sugar
juice of 1 orange

For the gingerbread ice-cream, crumble the honey cake into a bowl. Bring the milk to the boil with the spices and vanilla bean. Allow to infuse for 15 minutes. Strain onto the cake and leave for a further 10 minutes. Whisk this mixture to remove any lumps. If any lumps remain whiz quickly with a stick blender or in a food processor.

Beat the honey and sugar into the egg yolks. Return the milk mixture to a wide-bottomed saucepan and reheat, whisking all the time or it will stick. When it feels hot to your finger, pour onto the egg yolks, whisking as you go. Return to the pan and cook over medium heat, stirring until it reaches 80°C (175°F). Strain and allow to cool completely before adding the cream. Churn in an ice-cream machine according to the manufacturer's instructions.

For the spice syrup, melt the butter in a saucepan, add the ginger, cinnamon and a split and scraped vanilla bean. Sprinkle in the sugar and stir until dissolved. Add the orange juice and bring to the boil. Remove from the heat and allow to stand for 30 minutes.

Peel the pineapple carefully, removing all the eyes. Cut lengthwise into 8 pieces and then into even chunks. Reheat the spice syrup and strain over the pineapple. Set aside until needed.

Prepare the puff pastry following the instructions on page 154. Divide the pastry into 4 and roll out each piece to a thickness of 4mm (⅛ in). From each piece of pastry cut out two 10cm (4 in) circles and from the middle of each circle cut out a 3cm (1in) hole. Refrigerate the circles for 30 minutes. Prick the base with a fork.

Preheat the oven to 200°C (400°F/Gas mark 6). Remove the pineapple pieces from the syrup and drain on kitchen paper.

Arrange the pineapple on the pastry rings, and place the tarts on a lined baking tray. Dust heavily with icing sugar and bake until they are golden brown and slightly caramelised, about 8 minutes.

Reduce the syrup by half for the sauce.

To serve, place a tart in the middle of each plate and drizzle some syrup around. Place a scoop of ice-cream in the cavity and serve immediately.

Serves 4

SPICED PINEAPPLE TART WITH GINGERBREAD ICECREAM

An ambrosial union of ingredients that recall their ancient origins. The dish is dressed this way so that diners can enjoy the honey cream, sticky jellied quince and crunchy biscuit with every spoonful.

150g (5 oz) icing sugar
¼ quantity Puff Pastry (page 154)

Quince Syrup
600g (1 lb 5 oz) caster sugar
1 litre (2 pints/4 cups) water
375ml (13 fl oz/1½ cups) Sauternes
2 cinnamon sticks
3 cloves
zest of 2 oranges
6 quinces, peeled, quartered and cored

Honey Cream
500ml (18 fl oz/2 cups) cream
65g (2¼ oz) honey
40g (1½ oz) caster sugar
5 egg yolks
1 leaf gelatine, soaked in cold water

Sabayon
40ml (1½ fl oz) Sauternes or very sticky wine
¼ leaf gelatine, soaked in cold water
80g (2¾ oz) Pâte à Bombe (page 154)
110ml (4 fl oz) whipped cream

For the quince syrup, bring the sugar, water, Sauternes, spices and zest to the boil. Drop in the quinces and reduce the heat to barely a simmer. Poach on very low heat for about 4 hours or until the quinces are a deep red. Allow to cool in the syrup.

For the honey cream, bring the cream and honey to the boil. Whisk the sugar into the egg yolks until pale and thick. Whisk in the cream and return to the pan. Cook over moderate heat until the mixture coats the back of a spoon. Stir in the gelatine, strain and allow to cool. Refrigerate.

For the sabayon, heat the Sauternes until nearly boiling, then mix in the gelatine. Allow to cool, then whisk into the bombe mixture. Fold in the cream and refrigerate.

Preheat the oven to 220°C (425°F/Gas mark 7).

Dust a work surface with icing sugar. Cut the puff pastry into 2 pieces and roll out each piece into a rectangle about 20cm x 15cm (8 in x 6 in) and 3mm (⅛ in) thick. Dust heavily with icing sugar then roll up into a cylinder. From this cut 1cm (½ in) lozenges (work quickly as everything will become very sticky). Dust each piece with more icing sugar and roll, flat side up, very thinly. Cut into desired shapes and place on baking paper on a heavy baking tray. Bake in batches for 5 to 6 minutes. They will distort as they cook. Once golden brown, remove from the oven and press each one flat with the base of a saucepan. You will need 3 feuillantines per person.

To serve, sandwich between the three feuillantines alternating spoonfuls of honey cream and quince. Serve with the sabayon and a little of the quince poaching liquor on the side.

Serves 4

FEUILLAN-TINE OF QUINCE AND HONEY CREAM WITH SAUTERNES SABAYON

The dried fruit overtones of the Pur Caraibe chocolate complement perfectly the classic marriage of prune and Armagnac. The prunes for this sweet should be prepared at least two days in advance.

8 prunes, roughly chopped
8 x 6.5cm (2 1/2 in) rounds of
  Chocolate Sponge (page 154)

Delice
80g (2 3/4 oz) caster sugar
4 teaspoons water
1 egg
2 egg yolks
180g (6 1/2 oz) Valrhona
  Pur Caraibe chocolate,
  finely chopped, melted
  and kept warm
250ml (9 fl oz/1 cup) lightly
  whipped cream

Prunes
200g (7 oz) unpitted prunes
600g (1 lb 5 oz) caster sugar
1 litre (2 pints/4 cups) water
40ml (1 1/2 fl oz) Armagnac

Chocolate Sorbet
400ml (14 fl oz) water
100ml (3 1/2 fl oz) milk
120g (4 1/4 oz) caster sugar
60ml (2 fl oz/1/4 cup) liquid
  glucose
120g (4 1/4 oz) Pur Caraibe
  chocolate, chopped

Armagnac Ice-cream
100ml (3 1/2 fl oz) milk
400ml (14 fl oz) cream
100g (3 1/2 oz) caster sugar
6 egg yolks
50ml (1 3/4 fl oz) Armagnac
100ml (3 1/2 fl oz) cream
  (extra)

You will need eight 6 1/2 cm (2 1/2 in) dessert rounds that are 3cm (1 1/2 in) deep for this recipe. For the delice, bring the sugar and water to the boil in a small saucepan and cook until it reaches 115°C (240°F). At this stage begin whisking the egg and yolks. When the sugar temperature reaches 118°C (244°F) turn off the heat and when the bubbles subside, pour onto the beating yolks. Whisk until cool. Fold together the warm chocolate and egg mixture, then fold in the cream. Fill the rings with the mixture and refrigerate for at least 2 hours.

For the sorbet, bring everything but the chocolate to the boil. Pour this over the chocolate and stir with a whisk until chocolate melts. Strain and leave to cool. Freeze in an ice-cream churn, and churn 1 hour before serving.

For the Armagnac ice-cream, combine the milk and cream in a saucepan and bring to the boil. Whisk the sugar into the yolks until pale and thick, then pour the milk and cream onto the yolks, whisking continuously. Return to the pan and gently heat until it reaches 80°C (175°F) or is thick enough to coat the spoon. Do not boil. Cool the custard completely in a metal bowl. When cold, strain, then add the extra cream and Armagnac. Refrigerate overnight and churn in an ice-cream machine according to the manu-facturer's instructions 1 hour before serving.

Pour enough boiling water over the prunes to cover. Soak for 1 hour. Make a syrup with the sugar and water. Bring to the boil and add the soaked prunes. Reduce the heat and poach for 15 minutes. Remove from the heat and pour off half the syrup. Top up with Armagnac and refrigerate until needed.

To serve, press a chocolate sponge round on the delice. Run a hot knife around the ring and unmould the delice onto a plate. Put a prune and a scoop of chocolate sorbet on the plate and place a little chopped prune on top of the delice. On top of this (using a dessertspoon dipped in hot water) place a scoop of Armagnac ice-cream. Drizzle with some of the prune poaching liquid. Serve immediately.

Serves 8

DELICE OF VALRHONA'S PUR CARAIBE CHOCOLATE WITH PRUNE, ARMAGNAC, ICE-CREAM AND CHOCOLATE SORBET

STEP BY STEP SAVARIN WITH CITRUS FRUITS AND LEMON CREAM, SORBETS' AND FRESH BASIL

Citrus fruits are most definitely at their best in Winter, so make the most of the variety with this rich yet refreshing dessert. Mint can be used in place of basil if you like, and finish with some candied zest. The savarin can be made several days in advance.

1 quantity Blood Orange Sorbet (page 156)
1 quantity Pink Grapefruit Sorbet (page 156)
1 quantity Mandarin Sorbet (page 156)
a selection of citrus fruit: oranges, ruby and white
  grapefruit, mandarins, tangelos, blood oranges
12 basil leaves, cut into fine julienne
Confit Zest (page 156)

Savarin
225g (8 oz) sifted plain flour
1 teaspoon salt
20g (3/4 oz) caster sugar
10g (1/2 oz) fresh yeast
50ml (13/4 fl oz) warm milk (blood temperature)
3 eggs at room temperature, lightly beaten
130g (41/2 oz) softened butter

Lemon Cream
270g (91/2 oz) caster sugar
4 eggs
1 egg yolk
juice of 4 large lemons
finely grated zest of 5 lemons
175g (6 oz) butter at room temperature

Soaking Syrup
500ml (18 fl oz/2 cups) water
250g (9 oz) caster sugar
zest of 1 lemon and 1 orange
1 vanilla bean
1 tablespoon Grand Marnier

MAKE SORBETS

PREPARE GARNISH

Prepare the sorbets according to the instructions on page 156 and set aside until ready to use. Peel and segment the citrus fruits of your choice.

For the savarin, put the flour, salt and sugar in the bowl of an electric mixer fitted with a dough hook. Dissolve the yeast in the milk. With the machine on low, add the eggs and milk. Turn up the speed slightly and continue working the dough until you have a smooth, homogenous mass that forms a ball on the hook. Add the butter bit by bit. Keep the machine running until the butter is fully incorporated. Prove in a warm, draught-free place until doubled in bulk. Knock down and refrigerate the dough for several hours.

Divide the dough into 10 small pieces and in the floured palm of your hand shape to fit small kugelhopf or savarin moulds, or 1 large mould. Prove again for 45 minutes. Preheat the oven to 200°C (400°F/Gas mark 6). Bake the savarin for 30 minutes. Unmould carefully on to a wire rack and allow to cool.

For the lemon cream, whisk together everything but the butter. Transfer to a saucepan, and cook, whisking all the time until the mixture comes to the boil. Continue cooking for several minutes. Transfer to a bowl and allow to cool until just warm (about 40°C/100°F if you have a thermometer). Whisk in the butter piece by piece until all is incorporated. Refrigerate.

For the soaking syrup, bring all the ingredients to the boil and allow to cool. Arrange the savarins in a deep dish and spoon over the syrup. Leave to steep for 20 minutes then drain on a wire rack.

To serve, place a savarin in the centre of each plate. Surround with citrus segments and a little of the soaking syrup. Fill the cavity of the savarin with the lemon cream. Place a small egg-shaped scoop of each sorbet around the plate, scatter the basil and confit zest around.

Serves 4

SHAPE
DOUGH

SOAK
SAVARIN

SPRING

This cool pale green soup is basically an adaptation of the classic vichyssoise. The oysters and caviar add a touch of glamour.

1 cucumber, peeled and cut into long julienne
juice of 1 lemon
20 oysters, shucked just before serving
3 radishes, thinly sliced
1 teaspoon Osietra caviar
chervil sprigs

Soup

½ potato, very thinly sliced
500ml (18 fl oz/2 cups) Chicken Stock (page 152)
500ml (18 fl oz/2 cups) thickened cream
½ onion, very thinly sliced
½ leek, very thinly sliced
150g (5 oz) butter
500g (1 lb 2 oz) cucumber, thinly sliced
juice of 1 lemon

For the soup, boil the potato in the chicken stock and cream until cooked. Sweat the onions and leek in the butter until soft. Add the cucumber and sweat further. When the cucumber has wilted pour in the chicken stock, cream and potato. Boil for 2 to 4 minutes, then liquidise until smooth. Chill. Season with salt and pepper and add the lemon juice.

Wilt the cucumber julienne with a little salt and lemon juice.

To serve, place each oyster on a little mound of cucumber. Place the radishes on top of the oyster and top with caviar. Pour over the icy-cold soup at the last minute, and garnish with chervil sprigs.

Serves 4

CHILLED CUCUMBER SOUP WITH TASMANIAN PACIFIC OYSTERS, RADISH, AND OSIETRA CAVIAR

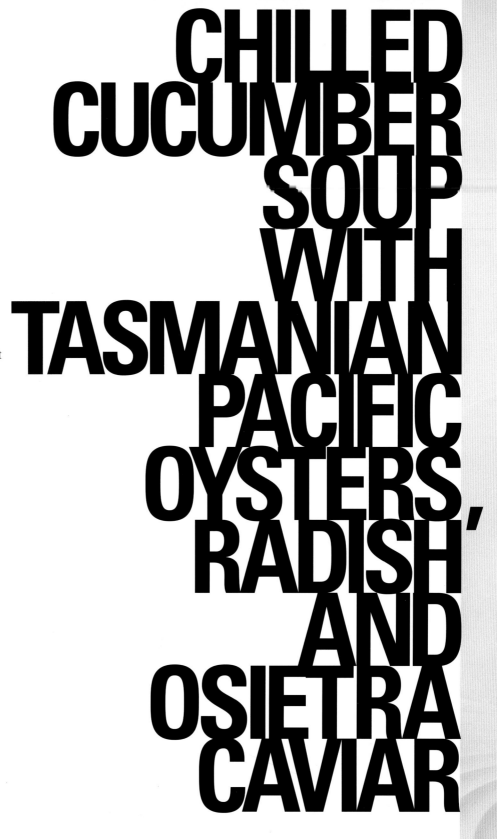

A loyal old friend, this adaptation of the Waldorf salad was on our very first menu and is now a mainstay of the menu at Luxe.

250g (9 oz) blue cheese
100g (3½ oz) Chicken Mousse (page 152)
200g (7 oz) Pasta (page 154)
2 crisp Golden Delicious apples, cut into fine julienne
4 sticks celery, cut into fine julienne
2 heads witlof, cut into fine julienne
50g (1¾ oz) walnuts, roasted
¼ bunch chervil

Vinaigrette
1 teaspoon Dijon mustard
100ml (3½ fl oz) walnut oil
50ml (1¾ fl oz) sherry vinegar
cayenne

Make sure that all ingredients and equipment are cold.

Place the cheese in a food processor and blend until soft. Fold through the mousse, making sure it is well mixed. Refrigerate.

Roll out the pasta through the thinnest setting of your machine into a long strip, then cut in half. Divide the mousse into 4 and place on one sheet of pasta about 10cm (4 in) apart. Cover with the second sheet of pasta, pressing down firmly to seal the edges. Cut out the ravioli using a round 6cm (2½ in) pastry cutter and pinch around to ensure a good seal. Blanch in rapidly boiling water until they float to the top and refresh in ice water.

For the vinaigrette combine the mustard, walnut oil and sherry vinegar. Season with salt, pepper and cayenne.

Dress the apple, celery and witlof with half the vinaigrette and place on serving plates. Finish the cooking of the ravioli, 2 to 3 minutes. Place on top of the salad. Scatter the roasted walnuts around. Drizzle the remaining vinaigrette over the ravioli and around the bowl. Garnish with chervil sprigs.

Serves 4

RAVIOLI OF BLUE CHEESE, SALAD OF CELERY, APPLE, AND WITLOF WITH A WALNUT VINAIGRETTE

This is just one of the many ways in which we combine fresh morel and asparagus. That their seasons overlap is opportune.

24 scallops, live in their shells

Risotto
2 shallots, finely chopped
100ml (3½ fl oz) olive oil
400g (14 oz) Arborio rice
50ml (1¾ fl oz) white wine
1 litre (2 pints/4 cups) Chicken Stock (page 152)
1 teaspoon grated parmesan
1 bunch chives, chopped
2 tablespoons whipped cream
24 asparagus tips
1 tablespoon olive oil
100ml (3½ fl oz) Chicken Stock (page 152)
24 small fresh morels

Scallop Stock
1 onion, chopped
1 leek, chopped
1 head garlic, halved across
2 sticks celery, chopped
scallop skirts
50ml (1¾ fl oz) white wine
400ml (14 fl oz) Fish Stock (page 152)
1 sprig thyme
50g (1¾ oz) butter
juice of 2 lemons

Open the scallop shells with a knife. Remove the skirts, discard the intestinal sac and coral and wash the scallops very quickly. Dry in a cloth. Wash the skirts very well as they tend to be gritty.

For the risotto, sweat the shallots in the olive oil. Add the rice and sweat for 1 minute. Deglaze with white wine. Reduce. Pour over half the chicken stock and cook for 6 minutes. Strain and spread the rice on to a tray to cool quickly, reserving the starchy liquid.

For the stock, sweat the onion, leek, garlic and celery in a little vegetable oil without colouring. Add the scallop skirts and sweat, then deglaze with white wine. Reduce by half. Add the fish stock and thyme and cook for 20 minutes. Strain, then reduce by half. Whisk in the butter and lemon juice to taste.

Return the rice to a pan with the remaining stock and a tablespoon of the starchy liquid. Cook for 4 to 5 minutes, stirring all the time. When the rice is cooked add the parmesan, chives and whipped cream. Keep warm.

Cook the asparagus in additional olive oil and chicken stock. Add morels 30 seconds before the asparagus is cooked.

Sear the scallops in a hot pan.

To serve, place a mound of rice in a serving bowl. Place the scallops on top, followed by the asparagus and morels. Pour the sauce around and serve immediately.

Serves 4

SAUTEED SCALLOPS, HERB, RISOTTO, ASPARAGUS AND MORELS

STEP BY STEP TORTELLINI OF MORETON BAY BUGS, AROMATIC VEGETABLES, ROASTED SHELLFISH SAUCE

If you cannot get hold of Moreton Bay bugs, use prawn meat instead.

36 Moreton Bay bug tails
1 egg white
300ml (1/2 pint) cream
zest and juice of 2 limes
leaves from 1/2 bunch coriander (cilantro), chopped
cayenne
1 quantity Pasta (page 154)
olive oil
1/2 bunch garlic chives, trimmed
a squeeze of lime juice

Garnish
2 carrots, julienned
1 celeriac, julienned
3 leeks, julienned
1 bulb fennel, julienned

Sauce
2 blue swimmer crabs, chopped into small pieces
2 tomatoes, chopped into mirepoix
roots from 1/2 bunch coriander (cilantro), chopped
100g (3 1/2 oz) ginger, chopped
1.5 litres (3 pints) Chicken Stock (page 152)
200ml (7 fl oz) cream
50ml (1 3/4 fl oz) Shellfish Oil (page 152)
a pinch of cayenne

MAKE FILLING

FILL TORTELLINI

Remove the bug tails from the shells. Trim the best 12 and reserve for the finished dish. Chop up the rest, putting half in a food processor and blending until smooth. Add the egg white with the machine still running. Season with salt and pepper.

Ensure that the ingredients and equipment are very cold. Add the cream and blend using the pulse button on the machine to ensure the mixture will not split. Add the lime zest, half the juice, half the coriander leaves and the remaining chopped bug meat. Season with salt, pepper and cayenne. Refrigerate for 1 hour.

To make the tortellini, roll out the prepared pasta bit by bit into very thin sheets. Using a 6cm (2 1/2in) pastry cutter cut out circles. Place 1 teaspoon of filling on the bottom half of the pasta round, and fold down the top to make a semi-circle. Press to seal the edge, then twist the 2 ends together to form a tortellini. Repeat with the rest of the pasta and filling. Blanch the pasta in boiling water for 30 seconds and refresh in ice water. Set aside.

For the garnish, blanch and refresh the carrots, celeriac, leeks and fennel. Retain all the trimmings for the sauce. For the sauce, sauté the crabs in a saucepan in hot olive oil until they smell nutty. Chop the celeriac, carrot, fennel and leek trimmings into mirepoix and sauté for 2 minutes in the same pan with the tomatoes. Add the coriander roots and ginger, then the chicken stock. Simmer rapidly on top of the stove for 1 hour. Strain the stock, reduce by half and add the cream. Bring to the boil, add the shellfish oil, cayenne and the lime juice.

Cook the tortellini in boiling water, season with salt and pepper and roll in a little shellfish oil. Sauté the garnish vegetables in a little olive oil. Add the garlic chives and remaining coriander, season with salt and pepper and lime juice. Heat the sauce and froth with the Bamix.

To serve place 3 tortellini and 3 bug tails on a serving plate. Put the vegetables in the middle and pour over the sauce.

Serves 4

TWIST
SHAPES

BLANCH
REFRESH

Hapuka is a deep-sea fish that goes well with molluscs. The sharp, fragrant sauce is very simple to prepare, yet the final presentation looks stunningly complex.

1 quantity Pomme Boulangère (page 98)

100ml (3¹/₂ fl oz) white wine
12 mussels
12 deep-sea clams (Tasmanian are best)
4 x 200g (7 oz) Hapuka steaks, skin on
6 tomatoes, blanched, seeded and diced
2 tablespoons chopped parsley
chervil sprigs
chive batons

A la Grecque
1 head fennel, cut into 1cm (¹/₂ in) dice
1 head celeriac, cut into 1cm (¹/₂ in) dice
2 carrots, cut into 1cm (¹/₂ in) dice
1 cup cauliflower florets
1 head garlic, cloves separated and crushed
10 black peppercorns, crushed
6 coriander seeds, crushed
roots from 1 bunch coriander (cilantro)
2 star anise, crushed
1 bay leaf
1 sprig thyme
200ml (7 fl oz) extra-virgin olive oil
2 tablespoons water
3 tablespoons tomato paste
juice of 4 lemons

Bring the white wine to the boil in a wide-bottomed saucepan. Add the mussels and clams and steam with lid on until they open. Remove the meat from the shells and set aside.

Prepare the Pomme Boulangère according to the instructions on page 98.

For the à la grecque vegetables, blanch and refresh the fennel, celeriac, carrots and cauliflower.

Combine the garlic, peppercorns, coriander seeds and roots, star anise, bay leaf and thyme in a food processor and blitz. Place in a piece of muslin and tie tightly. Put the olive oil, water, tomato paste and lemon juice in a pan, add the muslin bag and simmer for 5 minutes. Take off the heat and set aside. Remove bag when cold.

Preheat the oven to 260°C (500°F/Gas mark 9).

Pan-fry the hapuka, skin-side down, in olive oil until golden brown, flip over, then place in the oven for 4 to 5 minutes. Reheat the sauce and vegetables, and add the mussels, clams, diced tomato and chopped parsley. Spoon liberally around the plate. Place the potato in the centre and the fish on top. Garnish with chervil and chive.

Serves 4

ROASTED HAPUKA WITH MUSSELS, CLAMS, AND VEGE-TABLES A LA GRECQUE

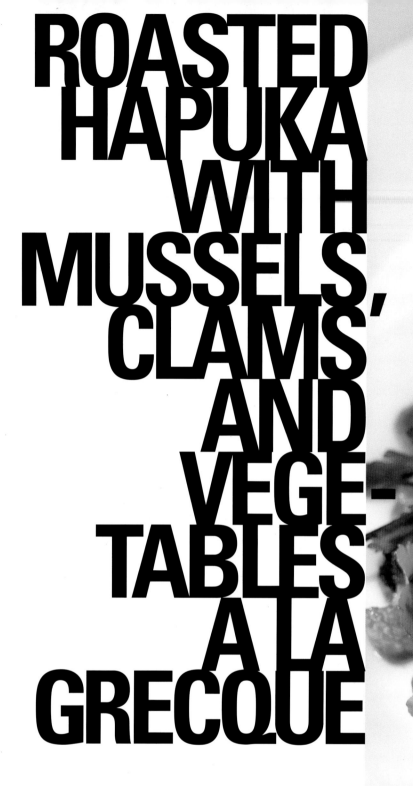

The keyword here is subtlety—the delicate texture and flavour of wild barramundi is enhanced by a light hickory smoking. All too often, the robust garnish or sauce served with this fish completely overpowers and dominates it.

2.5kg (5 1/2 lb) barramundi
100g (3 1/2 oz) rock salt
3 heads celeriac, cut into julienne
2kg (4 1/2 lb) snowpeas, cut into julienne
1 tablespoon butter
50ml (1 3/4 fl oz) water
20g (3/4 oz) Sevruga caviar
2 tablespoons Vegetable Nage (page 152)

Champagne Sauce
4 shallots, sliced
50g (1 3/4 oz) butter
100ml (3 1/2 fl oz) champagne
100ml (3 1/2 fl oz) Fish Stock (page 152)
100ml (3 1/2 fl oz) thickened cream
juice of 1 lemon

Fillet the barramundi, reserving all the bones and trimmings for making stock. Salt with the rock salt for 1 hour, then rinse in cold water.

Put the wood smoker on the heat. Allow the hickory chips to light, then cover with the lid. When the smoke dies down slightly, place the fillets, skin-side nearest the chips. Cold smoke—turn off the heat—for 30 minutes. (You can do this in a wok with the lid on too.) Once the fish has been smoked, cut into 180 to 200g (6 1/2 to 7 oz) portions.

For the sauce, sweat the shallots without colouring in the butter. Deglaze with the champagne and reduce to a glaze. Add the fish stock, reduce to a glaze, then add the cream. Bring to the boil, then strain. Season and add the lemon juice.

Just before serving cook the celeriac and snowpeas in butter and water. Steam the barramundi for 4 to 5 minutes.

Mix the caviar with the nage just before adding it to the sauce. Add the caviar to the warm sauce just before serving. Place vegetables in the centre of the plate. Top with the fish and surround with the sauce. Serve immediately.

Serves 4

LIGHTLY SMOKED BARRAMUNDI, CELERIAC' AND SNOW PEAS, CHAMPAGNE CAVIAR SAUCE

The relevance of this dish in spring goes without saying – if only milk-fed lambs were more often available.

1 x 6–7kg (13–15 lb) milk-fed baby lamb
2 bunches baby Dutch carrots, peeled and trimmed
2 bunches pencil leeks, trimmed
2 cups peas
3 bunches asparagus, trimmed
2 cups shelled broad beans
100g (3 1/2 oz) butter

Sauce
chopped lamb bones, roasted (about 2 kg/4 1/2 lb)
1 carrot, chopped
1 onion, chopped
1 leek, chopped
2 sticks celery, chopped
4 heads garlic, halved across
375ml (13 fl oz) Sauternes or a good sweet wine
3 litres (6 pints) Chicken Stock (page 152)
2 sprigs thyme
1 bay leaf

Gnocchi
500g (1 lb 2 oz) Desirée potatoes
70g (2 1/2 oz) plain flour
1 cup chopped fine herbs such as chives, parsley, chervil, tarragon

Get your butcher to break the lamb down into joints. (You may wish to use only one joint of meat.)

For the sauce chop all the bones into small pieces and roast in the oven until golden brown, 25 minutes. Sweat the carrot, onion, leek, celery and garlic in vegetable oil without colouring. Deglaze with two-thirds of the Sauternes, then reduce by half. Put the bones on top of the vegetables and cover with stock. Add the thyme and bay leaf. Simmer for around 1 1/2 hours. Strain. Just before serving, reheat and add the remaining Sauternes.

Preheat the oven to 260°C (500°F/Gas mark 9).

For the gnocchi, cook the potatoes (in their skins) in the oven on a bed of rock salt for 30 minutes, then scrape out the flesh. Pass through a drum sieve, knead in the flour, add the herbs and season. Shape into small dumplings, then blanch in boiling water and refresh in ice water.

Roast the lamb in the oven: the legs take 20 to 25 minutes, saddle 12 minutes, shoulder 8 to 10 minutes and rack 3 to 4 minutes. Rest for 10 minutes.

Cook the carrots, leeks, peas and asparagus separately in boiling water. Blanch and peel the broad beans. Melt the butter and toss through the vegetables.

To serve, carve the meat. Scatter the prepared vegetables and gnocchi around and pour over the sauce.

Serves 6

MILK-FED BABY LAMB, SPRING VEGE-TABLES AND HERB GNOCCHI, SAUCE SAUTERNES

Another of our old faithfuls, this ensemble of veal, sage and parmesan needs no introduction. Broad beans are at their best in Spring.

4 veal cutlets
500g (1 lb 2 oz) broad beans
1 tablespoon butter
24 sage leaves, julienned
50ml (1¾ fl oz) Chicken Stock (page 152)

Crust
11 slices white bread, crusts removed
12 sage leaves
40g (1½ oz) grated parmesan
1 egg yolk
200g (7 oz) butter
1 tablespoon cream
1 teaspoon Dijon mustard

Sauce
1 carrot, chopped into mirepoix
1 stick celery, chopped into mirepoix
½ onion, chopped into mirepoix
½ head garlic, halved across
150ml (5 fl oz) white wine
1 sprig thyme
1 bay leaf
I litre (2 pints) Veal Stock (page 152)
50g (1¾ oz) butter

Gnocchi
4 Desirée potatoes
a pinch of saffron
50ml (1¾ fl oz) Chicken Stock (page 152)
50g (1¾ oz) plain flour

For the crust, put the bread, sage, parmesan and egg yolk into a food processor and blend. Add butter, cream, mustard and blend until smooth. Roll into a cylinder 8cm (3 in) in diameter. Wrap in cling-film and refrigerate.

Trim the veal chops of any sinew and bone. Reserve the trimmings for the sauce.

Preheat the oven to 260°C (500°F/Gas mark 9).

For the gnocchi, cook the potatoes in their skins on rock salt in the oven until soft. Scoop the potatoes from their skins and pass the flesh through a drum sieve. Put the saffron in a pan and sweat in a little olive oil, then add the chicken stock and reduce. Add the saffron reduction to the potato, add the flour and knead together. Roll into a sausage and cut into 1cm (½ in) pieces. Drop into boiling water. When the gnocchi rise to the surface remove with a slotted spoon and refresh in ice water.

Blanch the broad beans in boiling water for 30 seconds and refresh in ice water. Pop the beans out of their shells.

For the sauce, sauté the meat trimmings, vegetables and garlic in some vegetable oil. Deglaze with white wine, and reduce completely. Add the thyme, bay leaf and all the sage stalks. Add the veal stock and simmer for 1 hour. Strain and stir in the butter.

Seal the veal on top of the stove in some vegetable oil, then put in a 260°C oven for 8 minutes until pink. Remove and rest in a warm place. Cut a slice of the crust and place on top of the chop after it has rested.

Put a little butter in a pan and heat until slightly brown, add the sage julienne then the broad beans, gnocchi and a little chicken stock and reduce to a coating consistency. Season with salt and pepper, then spoon this around the plate. Glaze the veal crust under a salamander or with a blowtorch or under a grill. Place in the middle of the plate, spoon over the sauce and serve.

Serves 4

PARMESAN AND SAGE-CRUSTED VEAL CUTLET, BROAD BEANS AND SAFFRON GNOCCHI, SAGE JUS

Choose the biggest and best ducks you can find for this unusual dish, and try each element together to get the full impact of its appeal.

2 x 1.8kg (4 lb) Muscovy ducks, legs reserved for ravioli
8 large heads witlof
100g (3¹/₂ oz) caster sugar
2 bunches English spinach
Confit Zest (page 156)

Ravioli
4 Muscovy duck legs
200g (7 oz) rock salt
1 head garlic, chopped
a few sprigs of thyme, chopped
1 bay leaf, chopped
1 litre (2 pints/4 cups) duck fat
150g (5 oz) Chicken Mousse (page 152)
100g (3¹/₂ oz) Pasta (page 154)

Sauce
1 onion, finely diced
1 carrot, finely diced
2 sticks celery, finely diced
1 leek, finely diced
1.5 litres (3 pints) Chicken Stock (page 152)
1.5 litres (3 pints) Veal Stock (page 152)
1 bay leaf
2 sprigs thyme
1 head garlic, halved across
1 cup crushed Arabica coffee beans
juice of 1 lemon
100g (3¹/₂ oz) butter

Salt the legs with rock salt, garlic, thyme and bay leaf. Allow to sit for 24 hours then wash in water and soak for 1 hour.

Preheat the oven to 80°C (175°F/Gas mark ¹/₄).

Melt the duck fat and submerge the legs in the fat and cook in the oven for 4 to 6 hours. Cool in the fat. Remove the breasts from the carcasses (reserve the bones for stock), discarding any sinew or fat.

Preheat the oven to 260°C (500°F/Gas mark 9).

For the sauce, chop all the bones into small pieces and roast in the oven until golden brown, about 20 minutes. Sweat the diced vegetables in vegetable oil without colouring. Place the bones on top of the vegetables. Pour the stocks over and bring to the boil. Add the bay leaf, thyme and garlic and simmer for 1¹/₂ hours. Strain. Reduce by half, then add the coffee beans and infuse for 1 hour. Strain again. Add the lemon juice and butter.

When the duck legs are cool take the meat off the bone, shred and add the chicken mousse. Roll out the pasta as thinly as possible and cut into 6cm (2¹/₂ in) rounds with a pastry cutter. Place 1 teaspoon filling on the bottom half of the pasta round, and fold down the top to make a semi-circle. Press to seal the edge. Repeat with the rest of the pasta and filling.

Sauté the duck breasts until pink.

Preheat the oven to 180°C (350°F/Gas mark 4).

Pan-fry the witlof until golden brown, then remove from the pan. Sprinkle sugar into the pan to make a caramel, then add the witlof and place in the oven. Turn every couple of minutes.

Cook the ravioli in boiling salted water for 3 minutes.

Sauté the spinach in some butter until wilted, season with salt and pepper.

To serve, place a mound of spinach on a plate. Carve the duck into 5 to 6 slices and arrange on top of the spinach. Place a head of witlof and 3 ravioli on the plate. Spoon over the sauce and garnish with confit zest.

Serves 4

ROASTED BREAST OF MUSCOVY DUCK, RAVIOLI OF CONFIT LEG, CARA-MELISED WITLOF, SAUCE ARABICA

A dessert that looks and tastes as though it's drenched in tropical sunshine.

1 quantity Pineapple Sorbet (page 156)
1 quantity Mango Sorbet (page 156)
1 quantity Banana and Passionfruit Sorbet (page 156)
mango, pawpaw, pineapple, melon, banana, passionfruit mint leaves

Pineapple Wafers
1 perfect pineapple
200ml (7 fl oz) Sugar Syrup (page 156)

Prepare the pineapple, mango, and banana and passion-fruit sorbets according to the instructions on page 156.

Preheat the oven to 90°C (200°F/Gas mark 1/4).

For the pineapple wafers, peel and slice the pineapple very thinly on a meat slicer if possible, but a Japanese mandolin or a sharp thin knife will suffice. Submerge the slices in the sugar syrup, place on a silpat mat and then on a baking tray. Bake for 2 hours or until crisp when removed from the mat. Store in an airtight container until needed.

Peel, slice and cut up the fresh fruit as desired.

To serve, arrange the fresh fruit decoratively around each plate. In the centre sandwich the sorbets one by one between the wafers. Spoon around some passionfruit pulp and garnish with mint leaves. Serve immediately.

Serves 4

PINEAPPLE, MANGO, BANANA AND PASSION-FRUIT SORBETS WITH TROPICAL FRUITS AND PINEAPPLE WAFERS

A classic, pretty combination of fruit, biscuit and cream, but with the dramatic assembly and the perfection of each element, it is lifted out of the ordinary.

½ quantity Sablé (page 154)
½ quantity Raspberry Sorbet (page 156)
1kg (2¼ lb) caster sugar
2 litres (4 pints) water
1 tablespoon Poire William
6 firm, ripe pears (Packham or Bartlett)
3 punnets raspberries
icing sugar
double cream
mint leaves

Roll out and bake the sablé according to the instructions on page 48.

Prepare the raspberry sorbet according to the instructions on page 156, reserve 100ml (3½ fl oz) for the sauce and churn the rest.

Bring the sugar, water and liqueur to the boil. Peel, halve and core the pears and place in the syrup. Press a circle of baking paper down on top of the pears and weigh down with a plate. This will keep them submerged and prevent browning. Reduce the heat to barely a simmer and poach until tender. Allow to cool in the syrup. (At this stage I usually soak the pears in some raspberry juice which I have as a byproduct from another dessert. It is quite expensive as it uses a lot of frozen raspberries. If you would like this effect, defrost 1kg/2¼ lb frozen raspberries, strain off the juice and add to the pears.)

To serve, place a sablé biscuit just above the middle of the plate. Slice the pears and layer them about 3cm (1½ in) high. Place another biscuit on top and arrange the raspberries on this. Dust the final biscuit with icing sugar and place on top. Decorate with a few raspberries. Spoon some raspberry sauce at the bottom of the plate. Place a small egg-shaped scoop of sorbet and double cream by the side, garnish with a mint leaf and serve.

Serves 4

SABLE OF PEARS AND RASP-BERRIES

As you spoon through the layers of soft cream, crisp nougatine and tangy sorbet you'll appreciate how good strawberries and cream really can be. A wonderful way to use the first strawberries of the year.

500g (1 lb 2 oz) caster sugar
1 litre (2 pints/4 cups) water
1 vanilla bean
1 bunch rhubarb,
  peeled and cut into 2cm (3/4 in) chunks
1 quantity Nougatine (page 54)
1/2 quantity Strawberry Sorbet (page 150)
100ml (3 1/2 fl oz) Strawberry Juice (page 46)
2 punnets strawberries, hulled and halved
mint leaves

Semifreddo
90ml (3 1/4 fl oz) milk
1 vanilla bean
grated zest of 1 lemon
2 egg yolks, beaten
250g (9 oz) mascarpone
3 egg whites
75g (2 1/2 oz) caster sugar
150ml (5 fl oz) whipped cream

For the semifreddo, bring the milk to the boil with the vanilla bean and zest. Dribble into the egg yolks, stir and return to the pan and cook over low heat until thick (do not boil). Strain into a bowl and add the mascarpone, stirring until smooth.

Whisk the egg whites until white and frothy, then sprinkle in the sugar and continue whisking until the whites are firm and hold stiff peaks. Using a whisk fold the whites into the mascarpone mixture, then fold in the cream. Freeze this in a 20cm x 30cm (8 in x 11 1/2 in) tray lined with baking paper. When solid, cut into triangles. Remove from the freezer and put in the fridge 30 minutes before serving.

Bring the sugar, water and vanilla bean to the boil and reduce for 5 minutes. Add the rhubarb and reduce the heat. Cook until soft, stirring gently. Then allow to cool in the syrup.

Prepare the nougatine according to the instructions on page 54 and cut into triangles.

Prepare the strawberry sorbet according to the instructions on page 156.

Prepare the strawberry juice according to the instructions on page 46.

To serve, arrange the cut strawberries in circles, cut-side out, in the middle of each bowl. Fill the middle with the rhubarb. Place a triangle of semifreddo on top, then a triangle of nougatine. Repeat the layers, then top with a small scoop of strawberry sorbet. Garnish with a mint leaf. Surround with strawberry juice and serve immediately.

Serves 4

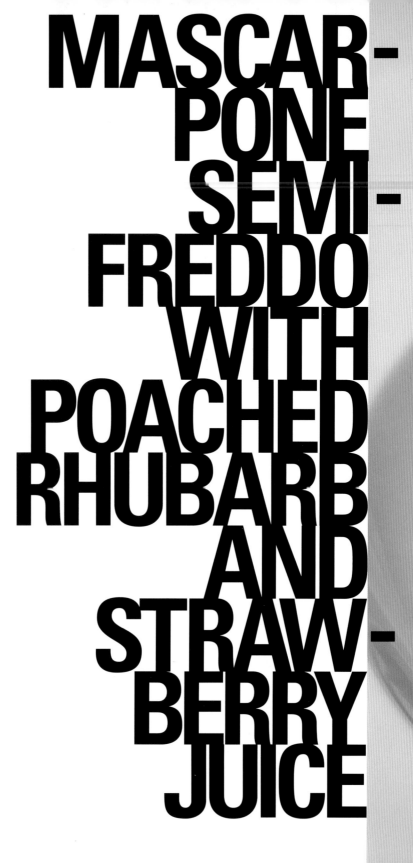

MASCAR- PONE SEMI- FREDDO WITH POACHED RHUBARB AND STRAW- BERRY JUICE

Celebrate the arrival of the first cherries with this rich, sophisticated dessert.

1kg (2¼ lb) cherries
80g (2¾ oz) caster sugar
1 tablespoon kirsch
2 punnets raspberries
1 quantity Raspberry Sorbet (page 156)

Pistachio Ice-cream
1 litre (2 pints/4 cups) milk
80g (2¾ oz) pistachio paste
10 egg yolks
180g (6½ oz) caster sugar
200ml (7 fl oz) cream
200ml (7 fl oz) kirsch

Cannelloni
50g (1¾ oz) sifted icing sugar
50g (1¾ oz) softened butter
50g (1¾ oz) egg white
35g (1¼ oz) plain flour

Using a small sharp knife or a cherry pipper, remove the stones from half the cherries. Set aside. Crush the remaining cherries with your fingers. (Don't lose any juice.) In a saucepan, combine the sugar and crushed cherries. Stir over medium heat until the sugar melts and starts to bubble. Add the kirsch and cook for 2 minutes. Set aside.

For the pistachio ice-cream, bring the milk and pistachio paste to the boil. Whisk well to dissolve the paste. In a bowl whisk together the egg yolks and sugar until thick and pale yellow. Whisk in the hot milk and return to the pan. Cook over medium heat until it reaches 80°C (175°F) or coats the back of a spoon. Strain into a bowl and allow to cool completely, then add the cream and kirsch. Refrigerate, and churn 1 hour before using.

Preheat the oven to 180°C (350°F/Gas mark 4).

For the cannelloni, using a wooden spoon, beat the icing sugar into the butter, then add the egg whites bit by bit and finally the flour. The mixture should be smooth and creamy. Using a palette knife, smear two rectangles about 12cm x 14cm (4½ in x 5½ in) on to a silpat mat. Neaten the edges with your thumb. Bake in the oven for about 8 minutes or until light golden. Remove from the oven and quickly roll the cannelloni around the handle of a whisk or a thick wooden spoon. Gently remove when set. (They will be very fragile.) Make the remaining cannelloni 2 at a time.

Strain the syrup off the crushed cherries and discard the cherries. Combine the pipless cherries and raspberries in a bowl. Add a little of the cherry sauce and toss to coat the fruit. Divide the fruit between serving plates and spoon around some of the sauce. Place 2 scoops of raspberry sorbet on each plate. Using a piping bag, fill the cannelloni with pistachio ice-cream and place on top of the fruit.

Serve immediately.

Serves 4

COMPOTE OF CHERRIES AND RASPBERRIES WITH A CANNELLONI OF PISTACHIO ICE-CREAM

BASICS

Chicken Stock

1.5kg (3½ lb) boiling fowl or an equal weight of chicken carcasses or wings, blanched and refreshed
200g (7 oz) carrots, left whole
white part of 2 leeks, cut into chunks
1 stick celery, coarsely chopped
1 onion, studded with 2 cloves
150g (5 oz) button mushrooms, thinly sliced
bouquet garni

Put the chicken or carcasses in a saucepan and cover with 2.5 litres (5 pints) cold water. Bring to the boil over high heat, then immediately lower the heat and keep at a simmer. After 5 minutes, skim the surface and add all the other ingredients. Cook gently for 1½ hours, without boiling, skimming whenever necessary.

Strain the stock through a wire-mesh conical sieve and cool as quickly as possible.

Makes 1 litre (2 pints)

Fish Stock (Fumet)

1.5kg (3½ lb) bones and white fish trimmings, cut into pieces
50g (1¾ oz) butter
white of 2 leeks, thinly sliced
75g (2½ oz) onions, thinly sliced
75g (2½ oz) button mushrooms, thinly sliced
200ml (7 fl oz) dry white wine
1 bouquet garni
2 slices lemon
8 white peppercorns, crushed and wrapped in muslin

Rinse the fish bones and trimmings under cold running water, then drain.

In a saucepan, melt the butter and sweat the vegetables over low heat for a few minutes. Add the fish bones and trimmings, sauté gently for a few moments, then pour in the wine. Cook until it has evaporated by two-thirds, then add 2.5 litres (5 pints) cold water. Bring to the boil, lower the heat, skim the surface and add the bouquet garni and lemon. Simmer very gently for 25 minutes, skimming as necessary. Ten minutes before the end of cooking, add the peppercorns.

Gently ladle the stock through a fine-mesh conical sieve and cool as quickly as possible.

Makes 1 litre (2 pints)

Mayonnaise

3 egg yolks
1 teaspoon Dijon mustard
400ml (14 fl oz) vegetable oil
50ml (1¾ fl oz) hot water

Place the egg yolks in the food processor with the mustard. Begin blending, drizzling in the oil slowly at the start until the mixture starts to thicken. As the emulsion thickens add a little water. Continue until the oil and water are all used up. Season to taste with salt and pepper.

Makes about 400ml (14 fl oz)

Veal Stock

1.5kg (3½ lb) veal bones, chopped
½ calf's foot, split lengthways, chopped and blanched
200g (7 oz) carrots, sliced into rounds
100g (3½ oz) onions, coarsely chopped
250ml (9 fl oz/1 cup) white wine
1 stick celery, thinly sliced
6 tomatoes, peeled, seeded and chopped
150g (5 oz) button mushrooms, thinly sliced
2 cloves garlic, halved across
1 bouquet garni, including a sprig of tarragon

Preheat the oven to 220°C (425°F/Gas mark 7).

Put the veal bones and calf's foot in a roasting pan and brown in the oven, turning them from time to time with a slotted spoon. When they are browned, about 30 minutes, add the carrots and onions, mix together and cook for another 5 minutes. Using the slotted spoon, transfer all the contents of the roasting pan to a large saucepan. Pour off the fat from the roasting pan and deglaze with the white wine, scraping up all the sediment. Set over high heat and reduce by half, then pour the wine into the saucepan. Add 3 litres (6 pints) cold water and bring to the boil over high heat. As soon as the liquid boils, reduce the heat so that the surface is barely trembling. Simmer for 10 minutes, then skim well and add all the other ingredients.

Simmer the stock, uncovered, for 2½ hours, skimming as necessary. Strain through a fine-mesh conical sieve into a bowl and cool over ice.

Makes 1.5 litres (3 pints)

Herb Pancakes

125g (4½ oz) plain flour
2 eggs, beaten
400ml (14 fl oz) milk
salt and pepper
1 tablespoon chopped chives

Place the flour in a bowl and whisk in the eggs. Whisk in the milk, salt and pepper and chives. Allow to rest in the refrigerator before use.

Makes enough for 8 pancakes

Chicken Mousse

3 chicken breasts, skin and sinew removed
4 egg whites
cayenne
300ml (½ pint/1¼ cups) cream

Refrigerate the bowl of the food processor for 30 minutes. Cut the chicken into pieces and process until smooth. Add the egg whites while the machine is still running and process until glossy. Season with salt, pepper and cayenne, then pulse in the cream. Refrigerate.

Poach a teaspoonful to check the seasoning. Adjust if necessary.

Makes 900g (2 lb)

Vegetable Nage

300g (10½ oz) carrots, sliced into rounds
white part of 2 leeks, thinly sliced
100g (3½ oz) celery, thinly sliced
50g (1¾ oz) fennel, very thinly sliced
150g (5 oz) shallots, thinly sliced
100g (3½ oz) onions, thinly sliced
2 unpeeled garlic cloves
1 bouquet garni
250ml (9 fl oz/1 cup) dry white wine
2 litres (4 pints) water
60ml (2 fl oz/¼ cup) white wine vinegar
10 white peppercorns, crushed and wrapped in muslin

Put all the ingredients except the peppercorns in a saucepan. Bring to the boil over high heat, then cook at a bare simmer for 45 minutes, skimming as necessary. After 35 minutes, add the peppercorns. Strain through a fine-mesh conical sieve into a bowl and cool as quickly as possible.

Makes 1.5 litres (3 pints)

Shellfish Oil

1kg (2¼ lb) shellfish heads (yabby, marron and crayfish only)
2 sticks celery, finely diced
1 onion, finely diced
1 carrot, finely diced
1 leek, finely diced
1 small bulb fennel, finely diced
2 tomatoes, chopped
2 tablespoons tomato paste
50ml (2½ tablespoons) Armagnac
50ml (2½ tablespoons) white wine
2 litres (4 pints) olive oil
1 teaspoon coriander seeds
3 star anise
1 vanilla bean
coriander (cilantro) roots, tarragon stalks, parsley stalks, chervil stalks, bay leaf, thyme

Chop the shellfish heads into small pieces. Sauté in hot vegetable oil until golden.

Sweat the diced vegetables in a pan in some vegetable oil without colouring until wilted and cooked—they should have a sweet smell. To this add the tomatoes and cook down, then add the tomato paste. Deglaze with Armagnac. Reduce and add the white wine. Reduce again.

Put the roasted shells into a pot and cover with the olive oil. Bring to the boil, then add the vegetables and the remaining ingredients. Put in the oven at 80°C (175°F/Gas mark ¼) and leave for 4 hours. Allow to cool, then pour into a bowl and refrigerate for 4 weeks. Strain and leave in the fridge for 1 week for the sediment to settle, then decant.

Makes 2 litres (4 pints)

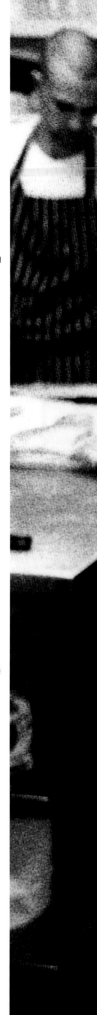

Pasta

500g (1 lb 2 oz) plain flour
a pinch of salt
8 egg yolks
3 whole eggs
20ml (3/4 fl oz) olive oil

Put the flour and salt into a food processor. Whisk the egg yolks and eggs together, turn on the processor and pour in the eggs. Add the oil and process until crumbly.

Tip onto a work surface and knead together. Wrap in clingfilm and rest for 2 hours. Roll out according to the recipe.

Makes 500g (1 lb 2 oz)

Chocolate Sponge

150g (5 oz) best bitter chocolate
150g (5 oz) butter, cut into small dice
80g (2 3/4 oz) egg yolks
120g (4 oz) egg whites
45g (1 1/2 oz) caster sugar
45g (1 1/2 oz) plain flour

Preheat the oven to 180°C (350°F/Gas mark 4).

Chop the chocolate very finely and melt gently over a bain-marie of barely simmering water. (The chocolate should be 40° to 45°C/100° to 113°F.) Add the butter piece by piece and stir with a spatula until amalgamated. Keep warm.

Whisk the egg yolks until pale. In a very clean metal bowl begin whisking the egg whites until they hold soft peaks. Sprinkle in the sugar and continue whisking until firm and shiny but not snowy.

Make sure the chocolate is still warm then fold in a third of the meringue. Work very quickly now lest the chocolate sets. Fold in the yolks and sifted flour followed by the remaining meringue. Spread the mixture onto a silpat mat or silicon paper and bake for 6 to 8 minutes. Cool on a rack.

Makes a 60cm x 40cm (24 in x 16 in) sheet

Tempered Chocolate

Chop the couverture with a heavy knife and melt in a metal bowl set over a larger pan filled with about 3cm (1 1/2 in) of boiling water. Remove from the heat after a few minutes, and stir gently until the chocolate is smooth and shiny, at 50°C (122°F).

Pour about four-fifths of the melted couverture on to a cool marble surface and work it with a large palette knife or scraper, continuously bringing it up over itself until it cools to 26°C (79°F). Scrape up the chocolate from the work surface and mix it with the remaining untempered couverture. Mix the chocolate with a spatula until it reaches 31°C (88°F). The couverture is now ready to use. Tempering will ensure that the chocolate hardens in a stable and shiny form. If it is not tempered, it will be cloudy.

Pâte à Bombe

180g (6 oz) egg yolks
150g (5 oz) caster sugar
75ml (2 1/2 fl oz) water

Place the yolks in the bowl of an electric mixer. Dissolve the sugar in a small saucepan with the water. Place over medium heat and cook until it reaches 110°C (225°F). When the syrup reaches 118°C (244°F) remove from the heat and allow the bubbles to subside slightly.

Pour the syrup in a thin stream down the side of the bowl. Whisk until cold.

Makes about 250ml (9 fl oz/1 cup)

Puff Pastry

This recipe for puff pastry was created by Jean Millet, and is the best one I know.

500g (1 lb 2 oz) plain flour
200ml (7 fl oz) water
2 teaspoons salt
2 teaspoons white wine vinegar
50g (1 3/4 oz) butter, melted
400g (14 oz) butter, well chilled

Tip the flour onto the work surface and make a well in the centre. Pour in the water, salt, vinegar and the melted butter. Work all the ingredients together with the fingertips of your right hand. Use your left hand to push small quantities of flour into the centre as the mixture tends to spread out.

When all the ingredients are well mixed, work the dough lightly with the palm of your hand until it is completely smooth. Roll it into a ball and lightly prick the surface with a knife to break up the elasticity. Wrap the dough in clingfilm and chill in the refrigerator for 2 to 3 hours.

Flour the work surface. Roll out the dough to make 4 'ears' around the centre. Put the slab of cold butter in the centre of the dough and fold up the 4 'ears' so that the butter is completely enclosed. Chill for 30 minutes.

Lightly flour the work surface, then gently and progressively roll the dough away from you into a rectangle measuring 70cm x 40cm (27 in x 18 in). Mark out the dough into 3 equal parts and fold the 2 ends towards the centre. This is the first 'turn'.

Turn the rectangle through 90° and again roll it out gently and progressively away from you, flouring the work surface as you roll. Roll out into a rectangle measuring 70cm x 40cm (27 in x 18 in), and fold over the dough once more into 3 equal parts.

At this stage wrap the dough in clingfilm and place in the refrigerator for 30 minutes to 1 hour. Repeat the above 2 turns. Rest for 30 minutes, then give the pastry 2 more turns, making 6 turns in all. Roll out according to the recipe.

Makes 500g (1 lb)

Biscuit Joconde

170g (6 oz) ground almonds
170g (6 oz) icing sugar
5 eggs
6 egg whites
30g (1 oz) caster sugar
50g (1 3/4 oz) melted butter, cooled
50g (1 3/4 oz) plain flour

Preheat oven to 260°C (500°F/Gas mark 9).

Pulverise the almonds and icing sugar in a food processor, then sift

Put the whole eggs in the bowl of an electric mixer. Whisk slightly, then add the sifted almond mixture and whisk at high speed.

In a separate bowl whisk the egg whites to soft peak stage, sprinkle in the sugar and whisk until shiny and firm.

Fold the butter into the egg and almond mixture, then fold in the flour. Stir in a third of the whites, then fold in the remainder. Spread on to a silpat mat or silicon paper. Bake for 2 to 4 minutes only until just firm to the touch.

Makes a 60cm x 40cm (24 in x 16 in) sheet

Pâte Sucrée

360g (12 3/4 oz) butter, diced
150g (5 oz) icing sugar, sifted
4 egg yolks
50ml (1 3/4 fl oz) water
500g (1 lb 2 oz) plain flour
a pinch of salt

Using an electric mixer fitted with the paddle or K beater, slowly work the butter until soft and even in texture. Add the icing sugar and mix together, taking care not to aerate too much. Combine the egg yolks and water and work into the butter.

Sift flour and salt onto a work surface and make a well in the centre. Put the butter mixture into the well. Gradually work in the flour to make a paste. Knead several times with the heel of your hand until smooth. Refrigerate for several hours before rolling out.

Makes 1kg (2 lb)

Sablé

500g (1 lb 2 oz) plain flour
400g (14 oz) butter (at room temperature)
200g (7 oz) caster sugar
1 egg yolk
1 tablespoon cream

Sift flour onto work surface and make a well in the centre. Put butter and sugar into the well and work until no hard lumps remain. Add egg and cream. Begin to draw in the flour and work until you have a mass resembling oatmeal. Begin smearing the mixture with the palm of your hand until you have a homogenous paste. Do not overwork. Roll pastry into a log and refrigerate for several hours before using.

Makes 1kg (2 lb)

For all the sorbets, measure the purée after you've sieved the fruit.

Pineapple Sorbet

1kg (2 1/4 lb) fresh pineapple purée
300g (10 1/2 oz) caster sugar
80g (2 3/4 oz) powdered glucose
280ml (10 fl oz) water

Combine all the ingredients in a saucepan and heat until the sugar has dissolved. Cool completely before churning in an ice-cream machine according to the manufacturer's instructions.

Makes 1.5 litres (3 pints)

Mango Sorbet

1kg (2 1/4 lb) fresh mango purée
360g (12 3/4 oz) caster sugar
100g (3 1/2 oz) powdered glucose
540ml (19 fl oz) water

Combine all the ingredients and heat until the sugar has dissolved. Cool completely before churning in an ice-cream machine according to the manufacturer's instructions.

Makes 2 litres (4 pints)

Banana and Passionfruit Sorbet

275g (9 3/4 oz) caster sugar
60ml (2 fl oz / 1/4 cup) liquid glucose
25ml (1 1/4 tablespoons) orange juice
425ml (15 fl oz) water
400g (14 oz) peeled bananas, ripe but not brown
500ml (18 fl oz / 2 cups) passionfruit juice

Bring the sugar, glucose, orange juice and water to the boil, stirring until the sugar has melted. Cool.

In a blender purée the banana and passionfruit juice, then stir in the cool syrup. Strain, then churn in an ice-cream machine according to the manufacturer's instructions.

Makes 1.5 litres (3 pints)

Pink Grapefruit Sorbet

1 litre (2 pints/4 cups) grapefruit juice
225g (8 oz) caster sugar
65g (2 1/4 oz) powdered glucose

Combine all the ingredients and heat until the sugar has dissolved. Cool completely before churning in an ice-cream machine according to the manufacturer's instructions.

Makes 1 litre (2 pints)

Passionfruit Sorbet

1kg (2 1/4 lb) passionfruit juice
360g (12 3/4 oz) caster sugar
170g (6 oz) powdered glucose
470ml (16 1/2 fl oz) water

Combine all the ingredients and heat until the sugar has dissolved. Cool completely before churning in an ice-cream machine according to the manufacturer's instructions.

Makes 1.5 litres (3 pints)

Strawberry Sorbet

225g (8 oz) caster sugar
75g (2 1/2 oz) powdered glucose
1kg (2 1/4 lb) strawberries, hulled

Place all the ingredients in a blender and whiz for 5 minutes until the sugar dissolves. Sieve and churn immediately in an ice-cream machine according to the manufacturer's instructions.

Makes 1.3 litres (2 1/2 pints)

Raspberry Sorbet

1kg (2 1/4 lb) raspberry purée
260g (9 oz) caster sugar
50g (1 3/4 oz) powdered glucose
120ml (4 fl oz) water

Combine all the ingredients and heat until the sugar dissolves. Churn in an ice-cream machine according to the manufacturer's instructions.

Makes 1.4 litres (3 pints)

Green Apple Sorbet

1kg (2 1/4 lb) Granny Smith apples
225g (8 oz) caster sugar
30g (1 oz) powdered glucose

Cut up the apples, core and all, and put through juice extractor. Measure—you will need 1 litre (2 pints/4 cups) juice. Add the sugar, glucose, strain and churn immediately in an ice-cream machine according to the manufacturer's instructions.

Makes 1 litre (2 pints)

Blood Orange Sorbet

1 litre (2 pints/4 cups) blood orange juice
220g (8 oz) caster sugar
30g (1 oz) powdered glucose

Combine all the ingredients and heat until the sugar has dissolved. Cool completely before churning in an ice-cream machine according to the manufacturer's instructions.

Makes 1 litre (2 pints)

Apricot Sorbet

300g (10 1/2 oz) caster sugar
85g (3 oz) powdered glucose
285ml (10 fl oz) water
1 vanilla bean, split (optional)
1kg (2 1/4 lb) apricots, stones removed

Bring the sugar, glucose, water and if using, vanilla bean to the boil. Add the apricots and boil for 5 minutes. Cool. Purée in a blender and push through a sieve.

Taste the mixture as you may like to add some lemon juice. Cool completely before churning in an ice-cream machine according to the manufacturer's instructions.

Makes 1.5 litres (3 pints)

Mandarin Sorbet

25g (1 oz) white sugar cubes
2 firm-skinned mandarins
1 litre (2 pints/4 cups) mandarin juice
200g (7 oz) caster sugar
45g (1 1/2 oz) powdered glucose

Rub the sugar cubes against the mandarins to extract the oils.

Combine all the ingredients and heat until the sugar has dissolved. Cool completely before churning in an ice-cream machine according to the manufacturer's instructions.

Makes 1 litre (2 pints)

Sugar Syrup

1kg (2 1/4 lb) caster sugar
1 litre (2 pints/4 cups) water

In a saucepan, bring the sugar and water to the boil, stirring occasionally with a spatula. Boil for about 3 minutes, skimming if necessary. Strain the syrup through a conical strainer and use when completely cold.

Makes 1.5 litres (3 pints)

Confit Zest

lemon zest
water to cover
Sugar Syrup (above)

This recipe also works well with oranges and other citrus fruits.

Using a vegetable peeler, remove the zest from the fruit. With a small, sharp knife, remove any remaining pith. Cut the zest into fine julienne.

Place the zest in a small saucepan and cover with cold water. Bring to the boil quickly, strain and repeat the process three times.

Cover with basic stock syrup and cook on very low heat for 45 minutes, topping up the syrup as necessary. The syrup should always cover the zest, and should never actually boil.

est est est is very classically orientated when it comes to matching food and wine. Often, characteristics in a particular wine are recalled, for example, a cured-meat character in a pinot noir may lead one of us to think of a certain rabbit dish, or a Pedro Ximenez of our chocolate soufflé. The sweetness of lamb may need the foil of a bolder cabernet. Often Philippa will try a wine and say that would be excellent 'with a dish' and it becomes a recommendation by the glass. Or I may recall an almondy characteristic in a riesling and know that it will be perfect with the new John Dory dish. I am most happy when, having ordered food, the order is shown to our sommelier so she can start thinking before she approaches the diner for the wine order. Sometimes a diner may say 'I am having a bottle of Mount Mary Cabernet 1988 — what should I eat with that?'. We are more than happy to make recommendations so that diners can enjoy the food and wine at their best.

With such a large and diverse wine list at est est est there are many rarities that guests will come back for, pre-reserve or have the remaining stocks set aside. We try to offer as much as we can, while holding the size to a manageable level. We also endeavour to list wines that are not readily available elsewhere, although there is some commercial content. We aim to offer an interesting choice that is value for money, and often list concurrently, for example, a Coldstream Reserve Chardonnay 1994 and a Coldstream Rising Chardonnay 1989. Usually the wines we buy are for the cellar and not the list; we purchase many things sight unseen. For example, we will take our allocation of Brokenwood Graveyard Hermitage regardless — it will be cellared and looked at over five years.

We have a very straightforward approach to what gets listed. Usually Leeanne and I go down to the cellar and have a wander around and a bit of a chat and 'grab' what we feel like. We might reverse our decisions by listing a wine and later deciding that it was too young after all and return it to the cellar. And often we will try, and like, a young commercial wine, regardless of fashion or policy. We have a very conservative approach to wine service and cellaring. Our cellaring facilities are perfect — underground, dark, stable and a constant 14 degrees (to within 1 degree) so that the wines remain in peak condition when they reach the table.

Frank Heaney

We would like to thank our loyal kitchen brigade that has supported us tirelessly through some very busy and stressful times. Thank you Josh Emett, Ben Russel, Karen Gay and Joseph Abboud. Thanks to our chefs Karen White and Rita Macali whose competence and dedication have left us confident to leave them to it at our other restaurant, Luxe. A very special thank-you to all our regular customers. We really appreciate your loyal support and hope we can continue to entice you. And lastly to Frank Heaney, whose front-of-house experience, wine knowledge and infectious enthusiasm for restaurants have made our partnership both enjoyable and rewarding.

Philippa and Donovan

Bamix A hand-held electric blender used to purée or beat foods until smooth or to whisk up liquids into a foam. We use this to lighten sauces for dishes and soups.

brunoise A term given to the cutting of vegetables into 1 to 2mm dice.

chocolate Valrhona is a very high-quality couverture that is available from specialist food stores. Pur Caraibe is a couverture made with cocoa beans from the Caribbean. It contains 67 per cent cocoa solids and has a spicy, dried fruit characteristic. Manjari is a couverture made with cocoa beans from the Indian Ocean. It is quite acidic, and has tropical and red fruit characteristics.

civet A stew made from game such as hare, venison, wild rabbit that has been marinated in red wine and cooked slowly for a long time.

clarify To remove the solid deposits from a stock using egg whites and vegetables, meat or fish. The egg whites coagulate, trapping all the solids while floating to the top. The raft that is formed is discarded.

compote Fresh or dried fruit cooked either whole or in pieces in a sugar syrup.

confit Literally, a conserve. The food is cooked very gently in fat or oil and then stored in the same fat or oil. Duck fat can be bought in tins from good food shops.

deglaze To dilute pan juices produced when frying meats and vegetables, using water, stock, wine or vinegar.

emulsion A preparation that results when one kind of liquid is dispersed in another with which it does not mix. An emulsion consists of a fatty substance such as oil that is dispersed in another, such as stock.

en vessie A pig's bladder in which chicken and other poultry are cooked. The bladder is sealed and put into stock or water at 80°C to slowly cook the bird in its own juices and thus intensify the flavour. We cannot get pigs' bladders in Australia. Instead, use two kitchen bags, one inside the other, and tightly seal the opening with string after expelling all the air. (If there is air the bag will float when you put it in the water.)

foie gras Goose or duck liver that is grossly enlarged by methodically fattening the bird with corn and maize. Only obtainable from France in a cooked form. It is expensive and can be purchased from specialist food stores.

infuse To steep herbs, spices or other flavourings into a hot liquid so that they impart their delicate fragrance.

julienne Food, generally vegetables, cut into very thin strips.

lettuce We use a variety of salad leaves, including mâche (lambs lettuce), mizuna, rocket and frisée (curly endive).

mushrooms Swiss browns look like button mushrooms and have a brown cap. Trompettes des mortes are French wild mushrooms that are available in dried form in Australia. Pine mushrooms are wild Australian mushrooms available during the autumn and winter months. Slippery jacks, also known as Australian ceps, are a wild mushroom from the boletus family. They are available during the autumn and winter months. Morels are a wild mushroom with a honeycomb-patterned cap that is available for a brief period in spring.

mirepoix A term given to a mixture of diced vegetables such as carrots, leek, celery, onion that acts as flavour enhancers for sauces, braises and stocks.

muslin Very fine loosely woven cloth used for wrapping foods or to line colanders or sieves for filtering liquid until very clear.

pavé Literally, a slab. Used to describe food cut into a neat shape, usually a shape or rectangle, for example, fish.

pine mushrooms, slippery jacks, ceps These are all wild mushrooms that cannot be cultivated and are seasonal. Available in autumn.

potatoes Bintje are a floury type of potato. Kipflers are small, long potatoes with an earthy flavour and semi-waxy flesh. Pink fir apple potatoes are also small and long, with a waxy flesh, ideal for salads.

quenelle Food shaped into an oval using a hot spoon.

reduce To boil a liquid in an uncovered pan. As the liquid evaporates the flavour becomes more concentrated.

sabayon A light foam made from egg yolks, wine and sugar and cooked gently over heat until the yolks start to thicken slightly.

sablé A crumbly biscuit made from a very short pastry. It must be individually rolled and cut.

salsify A root vegetable, also called the oyster plant. Two types are available: one is white skinned with many rootlets; the other is black skinned. Both are slightly bitter and strong tasting. Salsify is usually cooked in a *blanc*, which is water that has been acidulated then thickened with a flour paste. The salsify is then added and cooked slowly. The *blanc* will keep the salsify white.

sauté To fry food quickly in a small amount of hot oil. From the French word *sauter*, to jump, which the food appears to do when the frying pan is shaken.

savarin A ring-shaped gâteau made of baba dough without raisins. After cooking it is soaked in syrup and flavoured with alcohol or zest.

silpat mat A non-stick baking parchment that is silicon-coated. Prevents food and mixtures from sticking during baking. They are durable and reusable.

torte, pithivier These terms describe a sort of pie. Its filling has been wrapped in a pancake and then in puff pastry. The surface of the pastry is scored and baked.

truffle A subterranean fungus that lives in symbiosis with certain trees, mainly oak. Périgord in France is renowned for the best, but they can also be found in Italy, Spain and China. These fungi are totally unique in their aroma and their taste is like nothing else on earth. Their price is a reflection of this. The photo opposite shows truffles preserved in madiera and veal stock.

First published in Australia in 1999
by New Holland Publishers (Australia) Pty Ltd.
Sydney • Auckland • London • Cape Town

14 Aquatic Drive Frenchs Forest NSW 2086 Australia
1A/218 Lake Road Northcote Auckland New Zealand
24 Nutford Place London W1H 6DQ United Kingdom
80 McKenzie Street Cape Town 8001 South Africa

National Library of Australia
Cataloguing-in-publication data:
Cooke, Donovan.
    Marriages: Est Est Est cookbook.
    Includes index.
    ISBN 1 86436 444 0.
    1.Cookery, International. 2. Cookery (Game). I. Cooke,
    Philippa Sibley. II. Est Est Est (Restaurant). III. Title.
    641.59

Publishing General Manager: Jane Hazell
Publisher: Averill Chase
Additional text: Jenny George
Designer: Visnja Brdar, Brdar Design
Typesetting: Brdar Design
Separation: Colour Symphony Pte. Ltd.
Printer: South China Printing Co. Pty

EST EST EST COOKBOOK MARRIAGES

SHOULDER, FRESH NOO
EMON SAUCE, CHILLE
SUMMER BERRIES AND
OF APRICOT SORBET A
WITH SAUTERNES PO
BLACKBERRY AND LEM
GREEN APPLE SORBET
WITH A LEMON VERBE
TART. PYRAMID OF STI
PINK CHAMPAGNE PA
MELONS AND WILD S
OF SLIPPERY JACK AN
MADEIRA. MOSAIC OF
GRAS. RED WINE AND